The Brensham Trilogy
Brensham Village

John Moore was born in Gloucestershire in 1907 and educated at Malvern College. As he himself said, his half-hearted efforts in school and in business were always overshadowed by his keen love of nature study and his irrepressible passion for writing. He spent several years hitch-hiking round the world, writing freelance articles and short stories about his travels, including 'Tiger, Tiger' and 'The Octopus'. Many of his novels are set around Tewkesbury, where he lived for a major part of his life, and with books such as *Portrait of Elmbury*, *Brensham Village* and *The Blue Field* he made his name as an unrivalled chronicler of the English countryside. He died in 1967.

D1381492

Also available in the Brensham Trilogy

Portrait of Elmbury
The Blue Field

The Brensham Trilogy

Brensham Village

John Moore

Pan Books London and Sydney

First published 1946 by Wm Collins Sons & Company Ltd
This edition published 1971 by Pan Books Ltd,
Cavaye Place, London SW10 9PG
2nd printing 1976
All rights reserved
ISBN 0 330 02869 3
Printed in Great Britain by
Richard Clay (The Chaucer Press) Ltd, Bungay, Suffolk

FOR LUCILE

CONTENTS

AUTHOR'S NOTE

In *Portrait of Elmbury* I told the story of a market town in England's 'Middle West' during the period between the wars. Inevitably some of the neighbouring villages which were Elmbury's offspring and satellites came into the tale; and one of them was called Brensham.

Like Elmbury, Brensham is real in the sense that I have built upon a ground-plan and framework of truth: but I have purposely played fast and loose with chronology and topography and have not hesitated to make what Byron called a short armistice with truth in cases where it would have been embarrassing (to say the least of it) to write about living people. For example, I have transplanted a Lord, borrowed a Parson, and imported a Syndicate; and to that extent Brensham is a synthesis of the villages which lie about Elmbury and its biography is a synthesis too.

A few of the *Elmbury* characters reappear here: notably 'the Colonel', Mr Chorlton, and Pistol, Bardolph and Nym.

JOHN MOORE

April 1946

PART ONE

THE HILL

The Landmark – The Crack-brained Village – The Fabulous People – The Way to the Hill – The Mad Lord – The Bottled Crusader – Wild Wormës in Woodës – The Sugaring Expedition – The Hermit – Bird's Eye View – Fitchers and Gormleys – Christmas Holidays – The Syndicate – The Brief Loveliness – Brensham in Blossom-time

The Landmark

ALMOST every morning of their lives the weather-wise people of Elmbury lift up their eyes to glance at Brensham Hill which rises solitary out of the vale, four miles away as the crow flies. According to its clearness or mistiness they make their prognosis of the day; taking into account, of course, the season of the year, the direction of the wind, and the rheumaticky pains in their backs, their legs or their elbows. It is supposed to be a bad sign – in summer at any rate – to see Brensham Hill very plainly. If you can make out the jigsaw pattern of pasture and ploughing, stone wall and hedgerow, quarry and cart track, furze-patch and bramble-patch, and identify the stone tower atop which is called Brensham Folly, 'twill rain like as not before evening. If the hill appears as a vague grey-green shape, with the larch plantations showing as faint shadows like craters on

the moon, you can get on with your haymaking, for it's
going to be fine. But if you cannot see Brensham Hill at all,
if the clouds are right down on its seven-hundred-foot
summit, then you recollect the old rhyme:

> 'When Brensham Hill puts on his hat,
> Men of the Vale, beware of that,'

and you know you are in for a sousing.

Brensham, therefore, is as much a part of Elmbury's
landscape as the great Norman tower of Elmbury Abbey,
as the tall chimneys of the flour-mills, as the red sandstone
bridge which spans with four lovely arches the meandering
river. It rises up in front of you as you walk down the wide
main street; it appears behind the bowler's arm when you
bat on the cricket-field; it is the first landmark of home
when you approach Elmbury by train or car; and if you
glance round the corner of any of the alleys which compose
Elmbury's frightful slums its greenness against the sky holds
out to you a prospect of better things. From Tudor House
in Elmbury High Street where I spent my childhood I used
to look out across the flat green fields to Brensham Hill and
think of it as a mountain, its coppices as jungles, its slopes
as unmapped contours awaiting an explorer.

I had to wait a few years before I could simulate that
explorer; for our country roads ran less straight than the
crow flew, and a child's short legs couldn't manage the
distance. I suppose my nearest approach to Brensham in
those days was by river, for picnics by rowing-boat were
much in fashion and Brensham lay immediately upstream
of us, on the river's right bank. I remember my father and
my uncles in their shirt-sleeves, puffing like galley slaves as
they pulled the heavy boats, my mother and numerous
aunts in flowery dresses and picture hats, the yellow water-

lilies called Brandy Bottles hastily plucked in passing, the small hand trailed over the side and the pleasant sensation of water surging through the cupped fingers, the snowy tablecloth laid on the bank and the search for a site which was free from molehills, cowpats, or tuffets of grass, the usual alarm about wasps and cows, the heavy travelling-rugs: 'Wrap yourself up, child, it's so easy to catch a chill by the river.'

Once, after a longer row than usual, we reached the ferry at Dykeham, and Brensham Hill with its patchwork fields stood only a mile away. We might have actually picnicked in the water-meadows at its foot; but there was a high wind slapping little waves against the side of the boat, and we had with us an old and crazy aunt who announced that she was going to be seasick.

'How can you be seasick, Aunt Paddy, when you're not on the sea?'

'I can be seasick,' she said tartly, 'whenever I think I am going to be seasick.'

Alas, we knew this to be true; three old pleasure-steamers, the *River Queen*, the *River King* and the *Jubilee*, plied upon the river, and Aunt Paddy had even succeeded in being seasick when our boat rolled in their wash. So home we went, and Brensham Hill remained a distant prospect for another season.

The Crack-brained Village

By then I was a tough little schoolboy with three tough little friends, Dick, Donald and Ted, and a ferret called Boanerges, which I carried everywhere in my pocket, sometimes in company with a grass snake, to the discomfiture of both. We rode to Brensham, for the first time, on the bicycles which were tenth birthday presents, and thereafter spent most of our holidays there.

I had got to know Elmbury as only an inquisitive small boy can know the place where he is born and bred; so I was ready for further exploring. I had caught striped perch and loggerheaded chub in the rivers and streams which ran round Elmbury and through it, found larks' and curlews' nests in the big meadow called the Ham, climbed the four-hundred-odd steps to the top of the Abbey tower and gazed upon the coloured counties spread out below. I had achieved immortal infamy by scratching my name with a penknife on the sandstone wall of the Abbey. (It is still there.) And I had investigated, unknown to my parents, the rabbit-warren slums of the old country town and made friends with many of the curious and disreputable characters who inhabited them: with Slosher Hook, who waged war against his wife daily at the entrance to Double Alley, giving and getting blow for blow while the neighbours applauded and jeered; with Black Sal, who'd lost her wits and given up washing and who flapped about the town squawking and cackling like an old black crow; with numberless small ruffians who had filthy faces, ringworm on their heads, rickets in their bones, bottoms showing through ragged trousers, but who knew so much more about Life than I did that they seemed positively heroic. I also got to know those three musketeers whom I have since called Pistol, Bardolph and Nym. They were famous thieves, drunkards, beggars and scroungers who had served without distinction in various wars for what they could get out of it; they were just back from the Great War, and were already cocking a bleary and appraising eye at Peace to see what they could get out of that. They taught me a lot about rabbit snares and catapults, some merry rhymes, and some wicked swear-words; therefore they possessed in my eyes a sort of ragged

nobility of which time and riper experience hasn't quite
robbed them yet.

Now among the politer expressions which I learned from
these rascals, among the alley catchwords, the scraps of cant
and rhyming slang, and the old country names of things and
places which often sounded like, and sometimes were, the
uncorrupted speech of Shakespeare, there was a phrase
which made me prick up my ears as soon as I heard it: 'As
crack-brained as a Brensham hare'. Black Sal went flapping
by, and Pistol shrugged his shoulders: 'As crack-brained as
a Brensham hare'.

'Are there lots of hares on Brensham?' I asked eagerly.

'Lor' bless you, yes! Great fat lollopers! *We* knows!' He
winked at Bardolph and Nym, who repeated darkly:

'Aye, we knows summat about 'em!'

'What do you know?' I said.

'As they're good to yut,' said Pistol, grinning and rubbing
his belly.

'But why are they crack-brained?'

'All hares is crack-brained. Come to that, 'most everybody at Brensham is crack-brained. 'Tis a crazy place.'

'Tain't like any other village,' said Bardolph. 'There's
summat about it.'

'The folks is as wild as the hares,' said Nym.

'And very proud and independent-like,' put in Pistol.

'Three pubs they've got,' said Bardolph with a gleam in
his eyes.

'There's more drink drunk in Brensham,' said Nym,
'than anywhere else I knows of.'

'Fine upstanding women they have,' leered Pistol.

'And great folks they are for horses, and cricket, and dogs,
and boats, and fishing, and fighting and all kinds of sport,'
said Nym.

'They hangs together,' said Bardolph.

'Aye, they hangs together wonderful,' agreed Pistol. 'Pick a quarrel with a Brensham man and the whole village'll set on you.'

'Dogs and all,' said Bardolph solemnly.

'And they've got a Mad Lord,' said Nym.

'A real lord?' I asked.

'Aye. And mad. Crack-brained as a Brensham hare.'

The Fabulous People

So before I ever set foot in Brensham I already knew it as a remarkable and far-famed place, completely different in character from all the other villages and hamlets which ringed Elmbury and were her satellites. Upon the green slopes of the hill hares lolloped, Pistol, Bardolph and Nym slunk down the hedgerows, set snares, and were remorselessly hunted (if their tales were to be believed) by giant keepers with knobbly sticks and savage dogs; and there was a Mad Lord. There were also fallow-deer, we were told, which ran wild there, having escaped from his lordship's demesne. And if fallow-deer, what else might inhabit the place, what birds, beasts, butterflies, what hoopoes, what golden orioles, what fire-crested wrens, what polecats, martens, adders, lizards, Camberwell Beauties, Queen of Spain fritillaries, Bath Whites? I knew, already, my natural-history books by heart; and I peopled Brensham Hill with all the rarest creatures I could think of. It would not be at all surprising to discover Camberwell Beauties in company with a Mad Lord.

Moreover, there were other fabulous people besides the lord. There had been a murder in Brensham fifty years ago – the house where it had happened was still there, tumble-down and unoccupied, and was called the Murder House;

and the family of the murderer and the family of the murdered person still survived and carried on the ancient feud!
There was also a hermit, we were reliably informed, who
lived in the tower at the top of the hill – Brensham Folly –
and caught rabbits with his bare hands, and ate them raw.
And fabulous indeed was the Colonel, who had a farm at
Brensham and whom we saw almost every day, and usually
twice a day, as he passed down Elmbury High Street on his
way to the Swan Hotel. He rode, in those days, upon a very
old motor-cycle which made a peculiar and distinctive
chuffling noise. He sat up very straight, as he had doubtless
been taught to do in the Cavalry before the Boer War. He
wore a faded green jacket, knee-breeches, and a deerstalker
hat: a suit which, with trifling differences in the cut, might
have been made for Robin Hood. But his face, as much of
it as was visible between his chin-high muffler and the long
peak of his deerstalker, was not like Robin Hood's at all.
It was fire-red, save for the nose, which was purple. Below
the nose was a badger-grizzled walrus moustache, which in
winter became hoar with frost. Between the nose and the
peak of his hat one could sometimes see his eyes, which were
extraordinarily blue and twinkling. The general effect was
curiously elfin or gnome-like. His jacket had big poacher's
pockets which bulged with hares, rabbits, wild ducks and
pheasants in season, and at all seasons with bottles of whisky.

For it was whisky, whispered Old Nanny, hinted our
parents, declared with a leer lean spidery Pistol – whisky
that beckoned the old gentleman twice daily to the Swan,
sustained him in winter as he chuffled home in frost or snow,
revived him when he came back from wading knee-deep
through icy waters in pursuit of wild-fowl. It was the fire
from the bottle, they said, that burnt in his glowing cheeks,
the bottle was the paint-pot which decorated his purple
nose!

But we brats were no moralists. The Colonel was weird and wonderful, he belonged to the greenwood we were sure, he had some obscure affinity with Robin Hood. He was scarcely ever to be seen without some article of sporting impedimenta strapped to his motor-bicycle or slung over his shoulder: fishing-baskets, guns, salmon-rods, otter-poles, cartridge-bags, even rat-traps! In winter when snow lay on the ground he even appeared, on his way to stalk geese, in his sister's night-shirt, with a white night-cap on his head. It was said that when he failed to borrow a night-shirt he obtained a shroud and wore that. If such beings as he must feed on whisky, that only made them more marvellous in our eyes.

The Way to the Hill

Oddly enough, I do not remember the precise occasion when with Dick, Donald and Ted I first scrambled up the gorsy slopes of Brensham Hill. What I remember is a synthesis of many days we spent there during that first summer holiday from prep school.

The way to the hill from Elmbury took us through Brensham Village, which was long and straggling and ran in a semi-circle more or less coincident with one of the lower contours. The houses were mostly half-timbered, with deep straw thatch, and their gardens were full of old-fashioned flowers, hollyhocks and peonies, sweet-williams and rambler roses, red-hot pokers and love-lies-bleeding. There was a scent of gillyflowers which I remember still; so that whenever I smell it I think of Brensham.

There was a church with a tall spire, beside which three poplars grew, and spaced through the village at decent intervals there were three pubs, the Horse and Harrow, the

Trumpet, and the Adam and Eve. The Horse and Harrow, was locally spoken of as the Horse Narrow, which was confusing to strangers and had certainly confused the itinerant artist who had painted its inn-sign; for he had represented with meticulous accuracy a horse and an arrow. Nobody minded; nobody suggested taking the sign down and altering it, or making the artist paint a new one. The thing was a good joke; so much the better. That was the Brensham attitude and, looking back upon it now, I can see that it was typical of Brensham, where the people are humorous and tolerant and crack-brained and wise.

The Adam and Eve also had its painted sign. The artist this time had given full value for money; the tree, the forbidden fruit (undoubtedly a Cox's Orange Pippin), the serpent, the two naked figures, all were there in careful detail. If you looked closely you perceived that Eve's face wore a look of mischievous and disingenuous delight, not to say satisfaction; clearly, she had eaten the apple and enjoyed it. But there were some who said that the model for Eve had been the red-headed wanton little puss of a barmaid who served in the pub when the artist was staying there.

In the middle of the village was a turning off the road, called Magpie Lane, which led to the cricket-field and also to the Colonel's farm. Along this lane were a lot of little cottages which belonged to the Colonel; and I shall never forget my astonishment when I saw a number of small girls, who were the daughters of the cottagers, curtsy to the Colonel as he passed by on his motor-bike. He waved back, and his blue eyes twinkled. I had never seen a curtsy before; it was an enchanting sight, the small girls in their print frocks clutching the hem and bobbing, and the grotesque and wonderful old man waving back, at some peril to his stability, as he chugged by on his fantastical machine. It seemed to me entirely proper that he should receive these marks of respect; and I tugged hard at the peak of my school-cap as he went by.

Immediately opposite Magpie Lane was Mrs Doan's Post Office and Village Stores, which sold almost everything from fish-hooks to corn-plasters. The only commodities, however, which concerned us in those days were huge and tiger-striped bull's-eyes, so indestructible that you could use them for marbles, and elastic for catapults. Mrs Doan's elastic was very thick, and square in section; surely it must have been made specially for catapults by some manu-facturer with the heart of a boy, for I cannot imagine any other use for it. Nor, I think, could Mrs Doan; and since she strongly disapproved of the slaughter of birds, she had to invent an elaborate fiction to the effect that we employed our catapults for the purpose of shooting at tin cans. 'Now, remember, no *live* targets,' she would say. 'You will get just as much fun shooting at empty bottles; but you must take care not to cut yourselves with the broken glass.' Then she would quote to us a Victorian rhyme:

> *If Human Beings only knew*
> *What sorrows little birds went through*
> *I think that even boys*
> *Would never think it sport or fun*
> *To fire a nasty horrid gun*
> *Only for the* noise.

'Of course,' she would say, 'I know that catapults are silent; but this elastic is *very strong*, and if you hit a poor little fluffy bird with a stone you might hurt it *very badly*.' It was all we could do to keep our faces straight; we whose catapult handles each bore a score of notches. And I don't think Mrs Doan really succeeded in believing her tin-can fiction. She sold us the stuff reluctantly, rather in the manner of the

Apothecary selling the poison to Romeo: 'My poverty, but not my will, consents.' 'It's very *strong*,' she would say hesitantly. And so it was. The Elmbury shops sold nothing like it, and offered us instead strips of narrow pink stuff which might have served, we thought, for a girl's garters. We were shocked and insulted and thereafter we put up with her admonitions and dealt exclusively with Mrs Doan, whose square-sided cattie-lackey was as black as liquorice and so strong that when you pulled it back to have a shot you felt like a longbowman at the Battle of Agincourt.

The Mad Lord

When you started to climb the hill you left the half-timbering behind; the village still straggled along beside the steep path, but the cottages were built of limestone quarried a few hundred yards away, and the hedges gradually gave place to stone walls. Then you came to the end of the path and to the last cottage, which was inhabited by an old man with a wooden leg and a long beard. He kept in his garden a billy-goat which also had a long beard. We called him Goaty Pegleg, and thought of him as the hill's janitor, for he was almost always to be found leaning on the gate at the road's end. If he were feeling good-humoured he opened the gate for us; and we went through into a rough chalky field full of furze-bushes, ragwort, thistles and rabbits. A stony cart track led upwards towards the quarries, the banks covered with scrub and bramble, the hanging woods of oak, sycamore and ash, and the larch plantation on the hilltop, with the round preposterous tower of Brensham Folly just showing above the feathery tops of the conifers.

This was the unexplored jungle, the unclimbed mountain, the unmapped hinterland! (We didn't know what a

hinterland was but thought it must be some particularly
impenetrable sort of forest.) Off we scampered, with our
butterfly-nets, our rabbit snares given us by Pistol, to
maraud, to slaughter, and to explore.

How often the reality disappoints even proper explorers
of virgin lands! I suppose that El Dorado wasn't golden
when old tired Raleigh came to the bitter end of the dream.
But Brensham did not let us down; the hill which we had
peopled, as we sat in the nursery window, with fabulous
beasts and fabulous men did not fail us when at last we set
foot upon it.

There were no hoopoes nor golden orioles, it is true; but
there was a pair of merlin falcons, and before our amazed
eyes a *brown* jackdaw flew away among the black ones which
with loud clacking and chatter rose from the old quarries.
We saw no fire-crested wrens, but plenty of goldcrests in the
larch plantation. And there also, while we watched and
waited for we knew not what, we heard a patter as light as
falling leaves, and held our breath while three dappled
shadows cantered by, paused among the bracken, became
for a moment substantial in the sunlight as they twitched
velvet ears and noses, and then suddenly in a panic and
flurry of delicate legs rejoined the trees' lacy shadows and
so vanished. The Mad Lord's fallow-deer still roamed
Brensham Hill.

So did the Mad Lord. We saw him, I think, once during
the summer holiday. He didn't look mad; but he certainly
didn't look like a lord. He was dressed in an old jacket and
breeches which would have been moderately becoming
upon a scarecrow, and he rode upon a moth-eaten grey, an
ancient and decrepit bag of bones which the meanest of his
tenants would surely have sent to the kennels long ago. We
held open for him the wicket-gate into the larch plantation;
he felt in his pocket for pennies, found none, and gave us

instead a slow, gentle smile. We raised our caps, and to our
astonishment he swept off his hat, if it could be called a hat,
for like his jacket it would have served to frighten the rooks.
He rode slowly away and we stood amazed at his courtesy:
a lord had taken off his hat to us and smiled! He tittuped
down the ride, on his terrible mare which was rather like
Famine's mount in *The Four Horsemen of the Apocalypse*; and
it was four or five years before I saw him again. By then I
had read a book and I recognized a likeness; I knew that I
had seen Don Quixote riding on Rosinante.

The Bottled Crusader

The Mad Lord, whose wife had died, had a daughter of
about our own age, a pale-faced, wide-eyed, flaxen-haired
child called Jane whom we encountered from time to
time during our walks on the hill. She soon became
friendly and at ease with us, and one day she informed us, to our great astonishment, 'I have an ancestor
who lives in a sort of jamjar. I only show him to my special
friends. You can come and see him if you like.' We followed
her down by a rough scrambling path to the Mad Lord's
house on the side of the hill, where she obtained from her
easygoing nurse a large and important-looking key and led
us down the garden to a very peculiar building which she
told us was the private chapel. (It had been designed, we
learned later, by the second Lord Orris who had made a
Grand Tour and had been greatly impressed by Venice.)
She unlocked the door and took a candle and a box of
matches off the shelf. 'We're going down to the family
vault,' she said. 'Hardly anybody goes there except relations.' She held the candle above her head to light our way
down some wet slippery steps into a place of cavernous

darkness which was full of cobwebs and the rustle of bats
and which had a queer damp smell. At the far end of it was
an oaken door with a heavy padlock; she nodded towards
it and said: 'I've never been through there; but I know
what's in it. Can you guess?'

We said we couldn't.

'*Coffins*,' said our young hostess. 'But I expect they're not
worth seeing. They are all the dull ancestors. Robert, the
exciting one, is here.'

She lifted the candle to show us a small recess in the stone
wall, where there stood, not a jamjar, but a beautiful urn,
greeny-bronze in colour and very delicately fashioned.
Hanging on the wall beneath it was a framed inscription in
neat old-fashioned handwriting:

'This Urn contains the Heart and Viscera of Robert
La Bruère who fell at the Siege of Acre in 1191.'

Craning our necks we read above it another and later
inscription:

'There is a tradition that Robert La Bruère distin-
guished himself in the Third Crusade, and was at one
time a sort of aide-de-camp to Richard Coeur-de-Lion,
and eventually met his death in combat with Saladin
himself. His embalmed heart and viscera were brought
home in 1194 after the failure of the Crusade. Having
suffered various vicissitudes they were interred here in
1790.'

'What's viscera?' we asked.

Jane gave us a superior look.

'Insides,' she said. 'But his heart's there as well. For all
we know it might actually have a hole in it, where Saladin
struck him with his scimitar.'

It was our turn to be superior.

'Scimitars don't stick,' we said. 'They slice.'

'Well, then, with a slice out of it,' said Jane, tossing her head. 'Like a melon. Naturally we haven't looked. But I was allowed to hold the jar in my hands once. It was awfully light; but my father said: "Hearts weigh surprisingly light when courage and fear have left them." '

We began to think very highly of Jane. 'Well, that's that,' she said, in a businesslike tone. 'Goodbye, Robert.' She seemed to be on excellent terms with her ancestor. Then she held up the candle again and a bat's opening wings threw a huge and grotesque shadow on the roof, like that of a vampire; and Jane with scarcely a glance at it led us up the steps which were wet with green slime and showed us the way back through the garden gate. Another wonder was added to Brensham, which was surely the only village where you could find the heart of a crusader.

Wild Wormës in Woodës

We had peopled the quarries with adders; and sure enough among plenty of grass snakes and blindworms and a few swift darting lizards we found before long the exquisite poisonous creature with the yellow V behind his head. We never had any fear of snakes and I even tried the dangerous experiment of picking up an adder by his tail, and cracking him like a whip; thus, Pistol, Bardolph, or Nym had told us, you snapped his neck and he couldn't possibly hurt you. But my adder's neck was made of tougher stuff; he whipped back towards my hand like a piece of Mrs Doan's cattie-lackey, and I dropped him only just in time. After that we cut ourselves forked sticks when we went adder-hunting and used them to pin our victims to the ground. It was easy then to catch them behind the back of the neck and hold them prisoner while the forked tongue flickered out and the tail lashed back like a steel spring. One day as we held a snake thus we were astonished to discover that its belly was porce-lain blue instead of the usual yellowy-white. In other respects it looked like an adder; but we had never heard of a blue-bellied adder and we accepted it as another of the marvels of Brensham. We let it go, and afterwards searched through our nature books in vain for some account of it. Many years later, in an essay by W. H. Hudson, I read how the great naturalist had found just such a snake in the New Forest and how he too had let it go rather than slay it and coil it in a bottle for the learned consideration of the herpetologists whom he despised.

The Sugaring Expedition

Blue-bellied adders, brown jackdaws, merlins, fallow-deer – what more could we ask of Brensham? Certainly there were no Camberwell Beauties, but there was a Convolvulus Hawk Moth, which visits Britain rarely from North Africa and has a wingspan as wide as our largest native moth, the Death's Head. It sat upon a larch-trunk, resting perhaps after its long journey and awaiting its predestined captors; and we caught it with the aid of our prep-school master, Mr Chorlton, who had a holiday cottage on the roadside be-tween Elmbury and Brensham. This great man, who made us love Latin and Greek, had played cricket for Oxford and Somerset, had written a learned commentary on the plays of Aeschylus, now drank regularly a bottle of port each night after dinner and collected butterflies and moths with the enthusiasm of a schoolboy. Brensham was his favourite hunting-ground, and this in our eyes added to its glory. One

hot, still night in late August he took us up to the larch
plantation and taught us the game of 'sugaring' for moths.
Half an hour before, in the kitchen of his small cottage, we
had assisted at the ceremony of preparing the 'sugar'. Mr
Chorlton took off his coat and solemnly mixed the ingredi-
ents in a saucepan to the accompaniment of a running
commentary which, like all his talk, was as full of quotations
as a Christmas pudding of plums. 'First, black treacle made
by Mr Fowler. Not the same one who wrote English Usage,
perhaps, but a great man all the same: he makes thundering
good treacle. Sweeter than the lids of Juno's eyes or Cyth-
erea's breath. Now we add some brown Barbados sugar,
which I understand you brats call Niggers' Toes. You know
where Barbados is? It's one of the smaller islands in the
West Indies. When the news of the outbreak of war reached
Barbados in 1914 its legislature immediately cabled to
Whitehall: "Get to it, England; Barbados is with you." A
stout-hearted little island; no wonder it produces such excellent sugar. Now we stir the mixture. Double, double, toil
and trouble, Fire, burn, and cauldron bubble. Smell it.
Taste it if you like. Isn't it good? Isn't it a feast fit for an
Oleander Hawk Moth or a Clifden Nonpareil? But just you
wait. We pour it off into a tin; and now Monsieur Chorlton
the great chef completes his *pièce de résistance*. One or two
drops, see, of Old Jamaica rum. Nothing to beat it. Nor
poppy nor mandragora nor all the drowsy syrups of the
world. *Now* smell it! That's the stuff that makes the sailors
sing. That's the stuff that won the Battle of Trafalgar. Yo,
ho, and a bottle of rum!'

Then Mr Chorlton gathered up his net, his lantern and
his killing-bottle and we set off up the hill. It was dark when
we got to the plantation; the rabbits which scampered away
from our steps were disembodied white scuts, the first owls
were calling, the bats squeaked as they chased flies. Mr

Chorlton took a paintbrush out of his satchel and proceeded to smear the treacly mixture on the tree-trunks. You could smell the rum a dozen yards away. 'That ought to fetch 'em,' he said. 'One of the most endearing things about moths is that there are precious few damned teetotallers amongst 'em!'

When he'd finished painting the trees he lit a pipe and we waited beside the stile while the dusk deepened. It was tremendously exciting; for it was the first time we had ever been in the woods at night. We listened breathlessly to the scurryings and squeakings of small anonymous nocturnal things. Mice chirrupped; something – was it a blue-bellied adder? – rustled at our feet, something else went by in the air with a whisper of wings like a short gasp.

Gradually the darkness crept in upon us; we could almost see it advancing yard by yard, narrowing the circle. Mr Chorlton said something about 'the circumambient night'. He never talked down to us, never mitigated a phrase or a quotation to make it more comprehensible, but paid us the extraordinary compliment of supposing we should either understand or ask for an explanation. He always treated boys as if they were his equals; and this was not, I believe, a technique of his teaching but simply part of his all-embracing courtesy. Therefore we never thought of Latin and Greek as 'lessons' but as fun, like fishing and rabbiting and sugaring and learning the names of moths, which as it happened were composed of Latin and Greek words too. 'Lessons' were geography, taught by a parrot who repeated to us bi-weekly something he had learned by heart long ago about Isobars and Isotherms; or English, taught by a pedant who compelled us to 'parse' *the quality of mercy is not strained*; or History, taught by a fool who made us repeat Dates. But when Mr Chorlton discussed Virgil or Plato it was as much an adventure as being out in the woods at night; and we did not associate it with our desks and inkpots since he did it impartially both in and out of school. I still remember after thirty years the fragment from the *Aeneid* which he quoted to us that evening when our minds were set on moths and our young bodies were a-quiver with the novelty and the delight and the terror of the inward creeping dark. '*Nox atra cava circumvolat umbra,*' he said. 'Light the lanthorn! We'll see what visitors have come to our feast!'

Brensham on that occasion provided no rarities; but all was rare to us, as we followed behind the white beam and peered over Mr Chorlton's shoulder at the centipedes, woodlice, beetles, and huge horrific slugs which, as well as moths, were drawn to the strong-smelling sweetness. I think I remember an Elephant Hawk, its pink-and-olive wings beautifully incandescent in the rays of the lantern; and I am sure there were numbers of Red Underwings, great moths with forewings of delicately-shaded grey which they drape over hindwings of flaming scarlet; so that when the wings are raised for flight it is as if a dowdy old woman lifts her skirts to show the red flannel petticoat beneath.

However, we certainly didn't think of that simile at the time; for Mr Chorlton as always used the Latin name which was Linnaeus' lovely one, *nupta:* so for us it was a wedding-dress which the grey moth wore. When he spoke of creatures and flowers by their proper scientific names Mr Chorlton made us feel like men, or indeed like professors; so we did not trouble our heads with the English names but talked like naturalists from the very beginning. Thus we were enabled, at the age of ten or twelve, to disconcert a learned and pompous entomologist who came to give a lecture at our school. 'We call this,' he said, exhibiting a Cabbage White Butterfly – 'we call this *Pieris brassicae.*' 'So do we!' chanted four impertinent little boys in unison.

The Hermit

It was midnight when we finished the last round of the
sugared trees. Brensham Hill at midnight! – with the harvest
moon coming up through the black feathery branches of the
larches, and Brensham Folly upon the summit looking like
the Dark Tower in the poem! That was where the Hermit
lived; we should have been frightened, perhaps, if Mr
Chorlton had not been with us for the Hermit was a savage-
looking man, with a dirty grey beard, who bedded himself
down like an animal upon a heap of straw in the dark
cobwebby chamber beneath the Folly. And it was true that
he caught rabbits with his hands; he crept up to them where
they couched in the tufts of long grass and pounced on them
with a horrible pounce. (Thus murderers, thus assassins,
thus the following footsteps which suddenly begin to run!)
It was true too that he ate them raw, although we were
somewhat disappointed to discover that he skinned them
first. An eccentric old creature, as unhygienic as Black Sal
and even crazier, for he had made his own slum at the top
of Brensham.

How did he come to live in the Folly? It was said that he
had simply squatted there, constituting himself its unpaid
caretaker, and that the lord who was himself mad hadn't
the heart to turn him out. Local authorities were more
tolerant in those days than they are now, and Medical
Officers of Health rarely climbed up Brensham Hill; nor
would the workhouse have welcomed such a disquieting
inmate, for who knows what he would stalk and pounce
upon if rabbits were denied him? Certainly he was harmless
enough, he troubled nobody in his eyrie on Brensham; and
in summer, on Sundays and Bank Holidays when visitors
were to be expected, he even dressed himself up in an

ancient clerkish black suit, and a straw boater with a black-and-yellow ribbon, and conducted tourists up the steps to the top of the Folly, charging them a fee of threepence for the privilege.

The tower had been erected by an ancestor of the Mad Lord. It was large enough to contain a narrow winding staircase of stone leading up to the roof. A long inscription in bad Latin, carved spirally upon the interior wall, followed the course of this staircase so that the climber read it word by word as he mounted step by step:

UT TERRAM BEATAM
VIDEAS, VIATOR,
HOEC TURRIS DE LONGE SPECTABILIS
SUMPTU BUS
RICARDI ORRIS
DOMINI MANORII
AD MDCCLXV
EXTRUCTA FUIT OBLECTAMENTO
NON SUI SOLUM
SED VICINORUM
ET OMNIUM

We used to chant this as if it were a psalm as we climbed the stairs behind the Hermit, who for his part would always count the number of steps aloud, as if he wanted to make sure that there were always fifty-two. When we reached the top, puffing triumphantly *et omnium*, we entered a small dark chamber with slits for windows in which perhaps the altruistic Richard Orris had been accustomed to delight his neighbours with views of the blessed earth even on wet days. But now only bats inhabited the little room and slept, caring nothing for panoramas. When the trap-door in the roof was opened, letting in the light, they stirred uneasily with a slight dry crackle, like a crumpling of parchment.

The Hermit, observing with satisfaction: 'Fifty-two: that's as many stairs as there are weeks in the year,' would now insinuate his head and shoulders into the oblong hole where the trap-door had been and with grunts and groans would heave himself through it. Dick, Donald, Ted and I followed like a pack of pirates emerging from a ship's hold. Now we were on the roof. Upon the parapet another Latin inscription confronted us. From this elevated place, it said, when the sky is untroubled by cloud nor mists lurk in the low places thou canst see, O Traveller, twelve rich counties, four great cathedrals, and sixteen abbeys. There was a camera obscura which didn't work and a telescope with a broken lens. This telescope had the remarkable property of imparting to all objects seen through it the colour of bright yellow. Nevertheless the Hermit would put it to his eye and sweep it round in a gesture as proud as if he had been Nelson counting his ships before Trafalgar. When he stood thus upon the Folly roof the Hermit seemed to gain both in stature and in confidence. His beard and his long grey locks streamed out in the wind; he had something of the witless grandeur of Lear. He leaned upon the parapet, telescope to eye, slowly turning his head and reckoning up the counties spread beneath him nor caring, apparently, that they were yellow ochre instead of green. He smiled slightly with satisfaction, as a farmer who numbers his sheep and says to himself: 'Mine, all mine!' And then he beckoned to us and handed us the broken telescope and waved his filthy hand with its long talon-like fingers in lordly fashion as if to say: 'Mine, all mine; but you can look at them if you like.'

'Mine.' God knows, perhaps the poor crazy creature really thought so.

Bird's Eye View

We weren't very interested in the twelve counties, nor in the small smudge or speck which to the eye of faith represented a distant cathedral. We liked, it was true, to glance briefly beyond the serpentine Severn and the small silver glint of Wye to the mountains of Wales which looked Black indeed when the red sun was sinking behind them; but always before long our eyes came back home, to the roads we already knew and the lanes we were learning, to Elmbury among its fat green meadows and Brensham village among its leafy orchards.

Could we make out Tudor House where I lived, in Elmbury High Street? or Donald's house at the end of the town? Dick's and Ted's with lawns running down to the river? We often thought so; for there were the awful unmistakable alleys and slums, tight-packed tiny roofs which looked like rows of pigstyes (and, almost, they were). There was the cattle-market, an oblong open space which seethed like an anthill on Fair days. There was the Swan Hotel where the Colonel, if it was open, would be drinking whisky, and there the flour-mills with the rivers winding past them, rivers which wound about the town so crookedly that they seemed to tie it up in an untidy parcel. And there, rising over all, was the Abbey with its fine tower which always caught whatever light there was and glowed reddish-gold or tawny because long ago a great fire had enveloped it, marking it for ever where the red tongues had licked.

Then in search of more landmarks the eye crept back towards Brensham village, following the white unmetalled road which was our way from Elmbury to the hill, tracing our familiar route past the church with the tall delicate spire, the three poplar trees, the Horse Narrow, the Bell, Mrs

Doan's Post Office, the Adam and Eve, the railway station close beside it with the bright-glinting track running through it straight as a steel rod.

Look: the Colonel's farm. Ayrshire cows in the meadows, beautifully pied, hardly distinguishable sometimes from cloud-shadows; piebald horses; Gloster spot pigs; weird unfamiliar dappled sheep from Spain; a flutter of Plymouth Rock hens in the orchard – for everything that walked upon the Colonel's farm, including his dogs and even the cats, had to be pied. It was one of his fads, we were told. His house, like most of our houses, was half-timbered. His farm wagons, his drays, his larger implements, were painted cream-and-black. Even the petrol-tank of his old motor-cycle was striped like a zebra. Crazy, people said: crack-brained as a Brensham hare. But to us, as we looked down upon his Noah's Ark farm, it seemed entirely reasonable that a man should indulge such a pleasant whim if he wanted to.

These easy, simplified judgements of our elders often dismayed and bewildered us. There was, for example, the matter of the Mad Lord. Round the shoulder of the hill – you could only just see it from the Folly roof – was the big, beautiful Georgian mansion where he lived. The original Orris Manor had been burned down two hundred years ago; the present one dated from 1760. It was built in the semblance of a castle but with a grace and lightness which no genuine castle possesses; and it was tumbling down. Turrets and parapets were crumbling away, a chimney leaned drunkenly and some broken panes in the top-storey windows had been repaired with brown paper so that they looked like empty eye-sockets staring blindly down towards the village. Several trees were down in the park, the arch which bridged the moat had collapsed into the water, a dam had burst and turned half the garden into a bog. Nor was this

surprising for the moat had been made in the steep hillside
by damming a stream and contained its muddy water in flat
defiance of the laws of hydraulics.

It was incredible that a lord should inhabit such a ruin;
but when we inquired the reason we were told simply: 'You
see, he has no money.' That was another shock to us; we had
always thought that lords and great wealth were insepar-
able. However, it was explained that he had possessed some
money once, but he hadn't known how to look after it,
cheats and moneylenders had robbed him of it, rascals had
'borrowed' it, beggars had begged it; there was hardly any
left. Poor as a church mouse and mad as a hatter was the
Mad Lord Orris of Brensham. We asked wonderingly: 'In
what *way* is he mad?' and got the puzzling answer: 'You
see, he doesn't think money matters; he actually doesn't
mind being poor.' We pondered this *obiter dictum* and I am
glad to say that even at the age of ten we were able to see
the flaw in it. Our secret friends of the Elmbury alleys,
Pistol, Bardolph, Nym and their kind, hardly ever had a
penny to bless themselves with nor seemed to care for money
at all – whatever they got by begging and scrounging they
spent in the pub within a few hours; and yet it was apparent
to us that they were completely sane. Therefore, we reason-
ed, the Mad Lord was probably sane too; he was merely a
more eminent Pistol, a refinement of Bardolph, a lordlier
Nym. We remembered how he had swept off his hat to us
when we opened the gate for him, how he had smiled at us
as he rode away, and we decided that, mad or sane, he came
into our category of Special People, which included the
three musketeers, a bird-catcher who taught us how to make
bird-lime and set springes, Mr Chorlton, a professional
fisherman called Bassett, the Colonel, and the Hermit, who
was Special because he could catch rabbits with his hands.

Below the Mad Lord's unkempt park the land fell steeply

towards the river: apple trees gave place to old and crooked willows, which grew along the banks of all the ditches and beside the river itself. Brensham's cricket-field was here, on the very frontier between orchard and water-meadow: a light-green square with orchards on two sides of it and small sallows on the other two. Brensham was famous for its cricketers; it had given a dozen good players to the County team within recent memory. Its wicket was easily the best for miles around; better, some said, than Elmbury's, which was tended by two groundsmen and upon which two or three times a season the County played its too-serious games. The men of Brensham practically worshipped their smooth impeccable oblong in the square shaven field. Its High Priest was Mr Chorlton, who marked it and mowed it and spent much of his time kneeling upon it looking for offending daisies. An acolyte, the Brensham blacksmith whose name was Briggs, rolled it every Sunday morning as a sort of religious rite.

Not far from the cricket-field was a backwater of the river among osier-beds, with a landing-stage which was called the Wharf: the hay-barges used to take on their loads there in the days when river traffic went on. That had ceased long ago; but the men of Brensham, whose village was situated so curiously between the hill and the river, had never forgotten that they were watermen as well as hillmen. You could count a score of boats at the Wharf and there were others moored up and down stream, little groups of boats tied together so that they looked like the fingers of an outspread hand, long black fishing-punts, handy clinker-built tubs, mahogany sculling-boats for hire to visitors, two or three sailing-dinghies with red-ochre sails, some Canadian canoes, a precarious Rob Roy ... There were more boats pulled up on the bank for tarring or caulking, for mending or in process of building – for many of the Brensham men still made their own. They seemed to hold these craft in common; oars and rowlocks were always left on board and if you wanted a boat at Brensham you just heaved the peg out of the bank, climbed on board, and rowed away – if the owner arrived later and found his boat missing he simply borrowed somebody else's. Indeed it was regarded as unmannerly at Brensham to chain your boat to a tree with a padlock as people did in less happy-go-lucky places. However, this easy-going practice applied only among the natives; strangers, whom the Brensham men called 'foreigners' even though they came from only five miles away, must hire their craft from Sammy Hunt, who owned the cottage beside the Wharf and made his living in that fashion. He also owned the osier-beds, and cut the withies every year to sell them for basket-making. Sammy was rather a curiosity among the inhabitants of Brensham for he was a sailor born and bred and such as a rule like to settle down within sight of the sea; he'd been a Master in big tramp-steamers and small liners and had sailed all over the world. Yet here he was as near as he could get to the quiet heart of England, Master of no craft bigger than a fourteen-foot punt, with what must have seemed a mere trickle of water running past his cottage – you could throw a stone across the river easily – and the fat comfortable green fields all round him: like a land-locked salmon left behind by a flood. He still looked like a sailor, having a wrinkled mahogany face and sea-blue eyes, and he possessed a great store of tales about foreign parts and foreign peoples which he would tell you for hours while he caulked his boats or coiled down the painters all shipshape and Bristol-fashion in their bows.

Sammy had a sort of henchman called Abraham who helped him with his boat-building, and who wove the cut withies into baskets and putcheons for eels. Abraham also acted as ferryman, and would paddle you across the river in a tarry black punt for a penny. He was a sombre silent old man who had the rare trick of driving his boat through the water without the slightest sound. He never spoke, and sometimes on still foggy days when I have seen his long punt glide silently towards me out of the murk I have remembered uncomfortably as I stepped aboard it that there was another taciturn Ferryman whose fee was also a penny.

Upstream of Sammy's cottage was the Lock, and an old mill with a wooden water-wheel, which still ground corn; and beyond was another of our landmarks, the Murder House, a stark ruin, itself rather like something that had been murdered, with its blind glassless windows and its pale rafters like ribs showing through the broken red roof. We had explored it hesitantly at first, half-expecting to find bloodstains although fifty years had passed since the murder. A man called Fitcher had cleft the skull of a man called Gormley with a hatchet; and we played in a desultory way at being Fitchers and Gormleys, 'reconstructing the crime'. Soon, however, we heard a scrabbling in the attic, and Dick shinned up there to find a barn-owl's nest with two young birds. This interested us much more than any murder, and thereafter our concern with the place was purely ornithological. The villagers told us it was haunted, but we scoffed at them. 'The ghost is just an old barn-owl,' we said. Our curiosity about natural things was so large that we had none left over for the supernatural. *Dracula*, which we read about this time, bored us stiff; for we kept as a pet a real bat, captured in the Folly, and unbeknownst to our parents took it to bed with us, fleas and all.

Fitchers and Gormleys

The murder, after fifty years, might have been forgotten but
for the fact that both Fitcher and Gormley belonged to huge
gipsyish families whose numerous progeny refused to forget
it. The original quarrel, we were vaguely told, had been
'something to do with a woman' and Mr Fitcher, having
split open his rival's head, had sewn a quantity of lead into
his clothes and pitched him into the river. Soon afterwards
there was a flood, which carried the body down to Elmbury
where, as it happened, some of the man's relations owned
and operated a salmon-net. Heaving in this net, and remark-
ing that it was exceptionally heavy, they dragged out the
remains of Uncle Gormley, which must have been both a
shock and a disappointment to them, for he had been in the
river a long time and they had expected a draught of silver
salmon. Mr Fitcher was subsequently hanged; and the small
shrill children of the Gormleys thereafter would call out to
the Fitchers whenever they encountered them: *What's in the
salmon net today?* This rhetorical question was taken by the
Fitchers to be a deadly insult; indeed it was unwise to
mention salmon or nets in their presence. From time to time
a drunken Gormley would encounter a truculent Fitcher
and utter the fatal words; and then the trouble began.

Fortunately the two families did not often meet. The
Fitchers for the most part lived in tumbledown cottages on
the Brensham side of the hill; the Gormleys were encamped,
mainly in caravans, on the other side. Both got their living
in a precarious and gipsy-like way by hiring themselves to
farmers for seasonal work such as pea-picking and fruit-
picking; and since no farmer was so foolish as to employ
both families at the same time the risk of an encounter was
fairly slight. At Christmas-time, however, and especially on

New Year's Eve, the Fitchers and the Gormleys were apt to foregather simultaneously in the pubs of Brensham (whose landlords dreaded and hated them both impartially). There they would sit in separate groups, glaring at each other, and waiting for somebody to mention salmon-nets, or even accidentally to use any of the other words, such as 'hatchet' or 'rope', which were taboo because of their association with the fifty-year-old crime. This was sure to happen before closing-time, and then the Fitchers and Gormleys would stream forth into the peaceful village of Brensham like Montagues and Capulets into the streets of Verona. Both sides would call up reinforcements which appeared miraculously from nowhere; and for half an hour or so the running fight would go on all the way from the Horse Narrow to the Adam and Eve, the men punching each other, the women scratching each other, the small children biting and kicking. Nobody came to much harm, though the noise was terrifying; and the village policeman generally contrived to keep out of the way, knowing that his intervention was the only thing in the world capable of uniting the Fitchers and Gormleys, who would immediately make common cause against him. The sum of the damage was generally a few black eyes and bloody noses and some broken glasses in the pubs; the brief disturbance subsided as suddenly as it had begun, and the Fitchers and Gormleys relapsed into a state of mistrustful armistice until the season of peace and good-will came round again.

Christmas Holidays

We were the delighted witnesses of one of these battles, which occurred upon Boxing Day at the time when the pubs were closing in the early afternoon. A rout of Gormleys

came scampering down the road pursued by Fitcher males
with sticks and Fitcher females with umbrellas. Later, however, we discovered some small Gormley boys endeavouring,
apparently, to gouge the eyes out of some small Fitcher girls,
so honours were even. Shortly afterwards the Hunt came
galloping by and old General Bouverie the Master yelled in
a terrible voice to Gormleys and Fitchers impartially: *Have
you seen my fox, damn you?* and in a helter-skelter of red coats,
horses, shouting men, screaming women and children crying
What's in the salmon-nets today-ay? the whole fantastic riot
melted away and the violated village returned to its usual
mid-winter quietude.

Brensham in winter, apart from such occasional liveliness,
presented a workaday landscape; for the fields were full of
sprout-stalks which stank sulphurously as they rotted, the
orchard-trees were black and bare, the market-gardens were
littered with the left-over debris of late autumn, and the
smoke from a score of squitch-fires made blue streaks across
the land like smudged chalkmarks: a miniature industrial
haze. The river, every month or so, crept out over the water-
meadows, licked the bottom slopes of the hill, lapped the
doorsteps of a few low-lying cottages, and then sullenly went
back, leaving a brown scum on the fields. The people of
Brensham paddled about in gumboots and cursed their rich
dark soil which made such sticky mud.

But it would have taken more than mud to keep us away
from Brensham Hill, and we were up there, I dare say, on
the first day of the holidays and almost every day thereafter
for the next three weeks. However rough the weather or
sharp the season we never failed to find fun or mischief in
the quarries and coverts. Mr Chorlton, who was apt to call
us Beastly Little Barbarians, read us a passage from a very
old play, *The Play of the Wether*, which he said summarized
our whole attitude to life:

'Forsothe, sir, my mynd is thys, at few wordes,
All my pleasure is in catchynge of byrdes,
And makynge of snow-ballys and throwynge the same . . .
O, to se my snow-ballys lyght on my felowes heddys,
And to here the byrdes how they flycker their wynges
In the pytfall! I say yt passeth all thynges.

'That,' he would say, 'was written about 1540. It is a
sobering thought to an old schoolmaster that in spite of four
hundred years of education boys haven't improved one whit
since that time!'

Mr Chorlton, who detested winter walking, refused to
accompany us at this time of year. There were no moths to
lure him up to the larch plantation, so he stayed at home,
rearranging his collection, reading Aeschylus, Horace, and
the wine-merchants' catalogues, and drinking port. This
gave him his annual attack of gout which always lasted from
Christmas until the first butterflies came out at Easter.
Instead of him, we had for companions the bird-catcher,
Jim Mellor, who despite the Wild Birds' Protection Act still
carried on a profitable illicit trade in goldfinches; the fisherman Bassett, who took us live-baiting for pike whenever a
frost kept the river within its banks; the three musketeers,
who brought rabbit-nets and graciously allowed us to use
our ferret, Boanerges, to bolt the rabbits; and – most unexpectedly – the old Rector of Brensham, who turned out to be
a fine naturalist and was delighted to show us badgers' and
foxes' tracks when the first light snow covered Brensham
Hill.

This good and gentle clergyman, whose name was Mr
Mountjoy, remained sufficiently boyish at the age of seventy
to borrow our catapults for an occasional pot-shot at a sitting
rabbit or crow. ('I deplore blood sports,' he said, 'but you
can scarcely call it a blood sport if you never hit anything.')

He was not in the least embarrassed to be seen in the company of Pistol, Bardolph and Nym, who shamelessly used his cloth as cover for their poaching, disappearing into the bushes to set their wires and hastily returning to his side if the keeper came into view. 'What are you men doing up here?' asked a keeper once, knowing only too well. 'A-walking with His Reverence,' they growled. 'His Reverence invited us to come for a stroll.' For a long time we thought that Mr Mountjoy in his very great innocence was unaware of the three scoundrels' frightful reputation; we were somewhat surprised, therefore, when one day he turned to Pistol with a diffident smile and said in his precise way: 'I'm going to ask you a question and I hope you won't mind answering it to satisfy my idle curiosity: *What's the food really like in jail?*'

One of his hobbies was keeping bees. He had about fifty hives in his garden, and told us that their total population was nearly four million. 'That's as many bees as there are people in a great city. What a vast kingdom I rule!' On the first spring days he would stand contentedly for hours watching the workers sally forth and come back with the yellow crocus-pollen upon them; but at high summer he would often load some of the hives in the back of his small open car and go prospecting far afield for patches of beanflower or clover or saintfoin, and then beg the owner's permission to leave a hive or two there so that his bees could gather the honey. It was a familiar sight to see the Rector driving down the lanes with half a dozen skeps occupying the back seat while a little swarm of his turbulent passengers rose from them like a thin smoke and swirled about his head.

He was also a keen ornithologist. I suspect that Mr Mountjoy, like another and greater parson-naturalist, took more interest in his feathered parishioners than his human ones, was less concerned with his Easter sermon than with the arrival of various little migrants about that season. Certainly he spent more time in the fields and woods than in his church or rectory. He was inordinately fond of fishing, especially pike-fishing, and it was scandalously related of him that between christenings he would keep his live bait in the font. He was often in trouble with the stricter section of his congregation for offences of this kind; his church-wardens, for instance, objected to his fixing nesting-boxes over the church porch. They declared it was unseemly. 'My dear fellows,' said Mr Mountjoy, 'can you think of anything *less* sacrilegious than a pair of spotted flycatchers?' Some-times, apparently, his parishioners took their complaints to higher authority; for he confessed to us once: 'You won't see me tomorrow. I've got to go and take a wigging from the Bishop.' We feared greatly for him. 'I wonder,' said Dick, 'what the Bish will actually *do* to him?' But next day he was with us on the hill, unchastened and schoolboyish as ever, showing us the place where a hare ran through the hedge and telling Pistol with a wink: 'If you have any respect whatever for my cloth you will refrain from setting your wires until I am out of sight.'

The Syndicate

The keepers, whom Pistol, Bardolph and Nym delighted to deceive, looked after the northern face of the hill. The southern half, the side nearest Brensham, was owned by Lord Orris, who kept no keepers nor, had he done so, would there have been anything for them to keep. The Mad Lord's attitude to poachers was bewildering to respectable people and disconcerting even to the poachers themselves. If by chance he caught anybody unlawfully shooting his pheas-ants or netting his rabbits he would cheerfully wish them luck and apologize for having disturbed them. 'Carry on, my dear fellow,' he would say, 'and take what you can get. God knows, it's little enough that I possess which is of any use to anybody; but out of my pittance you are welcome to anything you can find.' Curiously enough the poachers resented this invitation, because it did not accord with their notion of how a landlord should behave, and they perversely went off and poached elsewhere.

But the northern side of the hill was preserved most rigorously. There were numerous keepers, there was barbed wire, notices everywhere proclaimed that Trespassers would be Prosecuted by Order, mantraps, it was said were illegally set in the coverts at certain seasons. Naturally we wanted to know the name of the landlord who was so jealous of his rights and so ruthless in the defence of his boundaries; but we were told that he had no name, the northern slope of the hill was owned by a Syndicate. Even then, before we understood much about it, or guessed what a dangerous threat this strange anonymous ownership held for Brensham, we felt that there was something sinister and unpleasant about a Syndicate. It had no face by which you could recognize it, no voice to greet you, no ears to hear your argument or your excuses. Even its habitation was not known. It came and went mysteriously: 'The Syndicate,' people said, 'is coming down from town this week.' Then you would hear an innumerable popping and banging in the coverts at the top of the hill. 'Ah, the Syndicate!' That was its only outward manifestation, that and the big cars with wooden-faced chauffeurs which swished by, hooting imperiously, whenever the Syndicate was about. But at other times its subtle and secret workings betrayed it, like mole-runs on a lawn even when there was no other indication of its presence. A man would be prosecuted for poaching and a lawyer whose face was unknown in Elmbury would get up in court: 'I represent, your worships, a Syndicate ... ' A hideous petrol-station was erected in a hamlet which was noted for its quiet loveliness. 'The Syndicate,' people said, 'put up the money.' And one day we found the gate into the larch plantation padlocked and surmounted by barbed wire. We hurried to tell Mr Chorlton. 'The Syndicate held a mortgage on it,' he said, 'and I suppose poor old Orris couldn't find enough money to pay the interest.' 'Tell us,' we asked him, 'exactly what a Syndicate is.' But Mr Chorlton was put out, and for once he failed to provide us with a ready explanation. 'Oh, a damnable thing,' he said, 'and there'll be no more sugaring in the larch plantation for us. But what's worse, I fancy it's got its claws into old Orris. Soon it'll put the squeeze on; and that'll be the end of him.'

But for a while the terrible Syndicate bided its time. Season by season the notice-boards which were its outposts advanced very slowly over the crest of the hill; the barbed wire and the keepers followed them, taking a field here, capturing a coppice there, as if they preferred to nibble away at the Orris land rather than gobble it wholesale. We came to think of the Syndicate as if it were some huge and shapeless elemental thing, *ingens et horribilis*, couched invisibly in the coverts above Brensham, looking greedily down upon the Mad Lord's ruined lands, licking its lips and awaiting the moment when it would pounce.

The Brief Loveliness

It was in January that the Syndicate bought or seized the larch plantation. (In subsequent years we noticed that most of the Syndicate's encroachments occurred shortly after Quarter Days, when the mortgage interest fell due.) At Easter we found the wood bristling with notice-boards and were smartly chivvied out of it when we entered in search of a goldcrest's nest. We got our own back by springing, next day, a number of open steel traps which the keepers had set for vermin.

That Easter was the first occasion when I looked down on Brensham in blossom. In winter, as I have said, and indeed for most of the year, the landscape was a workaday one. It wasn't a 'show' village; for although it had the same un-selfconscious good looks as all our villages had, its immediate surroundings spoiled it, because the rich soil had long ago been broken up into market-gardens. Consequently the cultivations were patchy and higgledy-piggledy; the assort-ment of crops included leeks, asparagus, cabbage, sea-green sprouts and emerald-green lettuces, tangles of raspberry-canes and rows of gooseberry bushes. Upon almost every patch were the small haphazard slums of fowlhouses, chicken-runs, pigstyes and toolsheds which grow up wherever there is market-gardening.

Between the patchy cultivations and among them stood the orchard trees which were the main source of Brensham's prosperity: apple, pear and cherry, but mainly plum. The orchards ran a little way up the hill and stretched all round it, a green hem to its skirt; they went nearly to Elmbury on both sides of the road; and they marched down into the vale almost as far as the river, stopping only at the green water-meadows which marked the limit of the winter's flooding. Surely there wasn't another parish in England which possessed as many trees!

Thus the people of Brensham, who looked out for eleven-twelfths of the year upon the commonplace and uninspiring spectacle of sprouts, cabbages and the like, were privileged for the remaining twelfth to live amid a scene of surpassing beauty. Upon a day between the last week of March and the third week of April the spring snowstorm swept up the vale.

For a fortnight or so the orchards were transfigured by this brief precarious loveliness, and people even drove out from the big towns on 'plum Sunday' to marvel at the prodigal blossoming. Before the frail plum-snow blew away, the lovelier bloom came out on the apple trees; and this was all the more exquisite because of the young green leaves which accompanied it. With cherry and pear, the apple blossom lasted for another week or two; then it faded, one day a fresh wind scattered the shell-pink petals and there was an end of May. Like a bride who packs away her wedding-dress and gets busy with her pots and pans Brensham went back to its green-and-brown ordinariness, taters, sprouts, onions, cabbages, beans and peas.

Brensham in Blossom-time

But on that Easter Sunday Brensham was dressed in white. The whole vale was carpeted with bloom under a dappled sky. It was a late season; the trees had all come out to-gether, ten million, twenty million boughs had burgeoned on the same blue-and-white April morning. The flowery tide ran up the slope of the hill for a little way and then broke, where the orchards thinned into a mere sprinkling, a spatter of silver-white spray. In the midst of all this loveli-ness, half-submerged by it, were the thatched roofs of Brensham; the airy spire of the church and the three tall poplar trees rose as if out of a flood.

We stood on the roof of the Folly; for it had become a kind of tradition that we should let the Hermit take us up the tower whenever we climbed to the top of the hill. He had put on his straw hat, a sure harbinger of spring; and he looked prouder and grander than ever as he surveyed the flowery scene through the telescope (which must have made the plum blossom seem as yellow as primroses) and, reckoning up the thousands of trees with their April promise of August wealth, dreamed no doubt that they were his.

How fortunate, I thought, were the people of Brensham, to live in such a village, their very roofs awash in the foam of the flowers! I was aware suddenly of the first curiosity about what went on beneath the thatched roofs. In Elmbury I had learned a little, perhaps more than my years warranted, about the teeming life which frothed and bubbled in the wide streets and the narrow streets, the crooked alleys and the tumbledown back lanes. But until now I had thought of people in terms of a pageant or a parade; the characters went by in endless procession, the merry ones, the solemn ones, the colourful ones, the drab ones, the respectable ones, the disreputable ones, the eccentrics, the fantastics, the drunks, the scroungers: all different, all fascinating, yet unrelated to each other. But now as I looked down from the Hermit's eyrie at the brown-and-yellow thatch of Brensham among the blossoming branches I had my first inkling of the existence of a community. From street-level you see only disconnected fragments, bits of the jigsaw puzzle, unrelated men and women going by; but when you see the roofs you see the place whole, houses, shops, pubs, churches, mills, gardens make a pattern and then the people who dwell in them, buy and sell in them, drink, worship, work in them, must surely compose some sort of a pattern too.

At all events, perched on the parapet with Dick, Donald and Ted while the Hermit surveyed his imaginary domain through the broken telescope which blurred all objects so that they appeared as misty and insubstantial as his dream, I perceived a kind of pattern in the straggling roofs of Brensham and my awakened curiosity about people was like a sharp pricking in my brain. I was possessed all at once by a huge inquisitiveness. Down there dwelt the

Colonel and the Mad Lord and the parson-naturalist and
Mr Chorlton, Sammy Hunt with his boats and his osiers,
the Fitchers and the Gormleys in perpetual strife, Mrs
Doan, the pub-keepers, the cottagers, the market-gardeners,
the labourers. Somehow I realized dimly that these ill-
assorted, contrary and individualistic elements formed a
community which perhaps was different from other com-
munities. At any rate I decided that I wanted to know
about Brensham, and about what went on under the roofs.

PART TWO

THE CRICKET-TEAM

Honorary Villager – The Cricket-ground – The Captain – The Secretary – The Blacksmith – The Potterer – The 'Boys' – The Drunkard – The Scorer – The Helpers – The Spectators – The Match against Woody Bourton

Honorary Villager

PERHAPS I should never have got to know much about Brensham but for the accident that I was not a very good cricketer. When I left school I returned to Elmbury and was articled to my uncle, who was an auctioneer. I joined the Elmbury Cricket Club, which played competent and rather solemn games on Saturday afternoons and which didn't take long to discover that my rightful place in the batting-order was last. But so competent and solemn were the earlier batsmen that they very rarely got out; and in practice I hardly ever batted at all.

Now Brensham, whose parson was tolerant and broad-minded (as was to be expected of one who kept live bait in his font), sometimes played cricket on Sundays; and one day Mr Chorlton invited me to join the team. The Brensham standard was not so high as Elmbury's; and I was put in fifth wicket down. Moreover the previous batsmen, whose approach to the game was light-hearted and happy-go-lucky

smote the ball hard, high and often so that before long
they were all caught in the deep. Within half an hour of
the start of the innings I found myself walking to the
wicket. This unfamiliar experience was so intoxicating that
I was heartened to swipe the first ball over the bowler's head
for six. The next one bowled me middle-stump; but I had
had my fun and I walked back cheerfully to the pavilion
where Mr Chorlton, Briggs the blacksmith, and Sammy
Hunt were chuckling and clapping. 'That's the sort of
innings we like to see at Brensham,' they said. After the
match we all went to the Adam and Eve and played darts;
and I drank more beer than a seventeen-year-old is supposed
to be able to carry. Sammy Hunt, who was the captain of
the team, invited me to play for it regularly; and since
whatever loyalty I possessed to the Elmbury Club had been
dissipated by beer I gladly accepted.

Thereafter, on Saturdays and Sundays throughout the
summer, I made my way to the small square cricket-field
which lay between the orchards and the river; at first by bicycle, later upon an old ramshackle Triumph, and once or
twice when the Triumph broke down, on horseback. The
spectacle of a young man in blazer and white flannels, carrying a bat, trotting down the village street on a lanky chestnut
didn't at all surprise the people of Brensham; for almost
everybody in the place was a horseman, and the neighbouring farmer's sons would often ride to the village dances
in white waistcoats and tails. And already I was accepted
as belonging to the village; for they had known me as a boy,
buying cattie-lackey at Mrs Doan's shop or wandering over
the hill where the keepers employed by the Syndicate spoke
of me and my three friends as 'they young Varmins'. In
the Adam and Eve after a cricket-match, an old man wearing the traditional velveteens came up to me grinning and
said: 'I knows thee. Thee be one of they young Varmins.'

So although I was technically a 'foreigner' (for I lived four miles away, and even the people of neighbouring Dykeham, just across the river, were considered foreigners) I was permitted a sort of honorary membership of the Brensham community.

Thus I got to know it and love it as well as I did Elmbury; I played cricket and darts, drank beer, sang in the pubs, fished, rode, shot and boated with the crack-brained people of Brensham until my ways became woven with theirs; and thus I learned gradually, sentence by sentence and paragraph by paragraph, the story of what went on beneath the roofs.

The Cricket-ground

I used to think that the cricket-field at Brensham, on a blue afternoon in May, must surely be one of the pleasantest places in the world; and certainly, when I travelled about the world, I found few places pleasanter. About the time of the first match, the apple blossom came out, and the willows put on their young green. The first cuckoo arrived and started calling from the small adjacent meadow which was appropriately named Cuckoo Pen. There were cuckoo-flowers in this meadow too, a silver-lilac carpet of them, so that we did not know whether it was called after the bird or the flower. Lapwings had their nests there, and sometimes we found the mottled eggs when we were looking for a ball which had been skied, Brensham-fashion, right over the tops of the willow trees.

To match the newness of the spring, Mr Chorlton had repainted the pavilion in green and white. Against the very fresh green of the pitch – the floods had lain on it for weeks at mid-winter – the white lines of the creases showed sharp and clear. And how white in the spring sunshine were the flannels well creased after months in bottom-drawers, the umpires' coats, the new-blanco'd pads and cricket-boots! How bright were the many-coloured blazers, and Mr Chorlton's harlequin cap, and Mr Mountjoy's I. Zingari! (Where else had I seen those colours? Why, round the battered straw hat which the Hermit wore when he showed visitors up to the roof of the Folly on high days and holidays. Mr Mountjoy must have given it to him!)

Smells and sounds: the sweet linseed smell of bat-oil, and an indefinable clean smell (waterweed and foam?) which came from the weir and the lock up-river. The gillyflower smell which blows in little brief gusts all over Brensham when there is a wind. The satisfying smack of a well-oiled bat hitting a ball during a knock-up before the game. The first bees buzzing in the apple blossom. And in the willow-branches ubiquitous the endlessly repeated *chiff-chaff*, *chiff-chaff*, *chiff-chaff*, *chiff*, of the little yellow-olive bird from across the sea.

Clatter of plates in the lean-to hut behind the pavilion: the Helpers were already preparing the tea. These Helpers were a personable lot: Mrs Doan's daughter Sally, the young wife of the landlord of the Adam and Eve, and two merry little blondes, Mimi and Meg, from the Horse Narrow. We were proud of them, because they always excited the wonder and admiration of visiting teams. We were also proud of their teas, which were not teas in the sedate drawing-room sense, but were more like Hunt Breakfasts, for they consisted of home-made meat-pies, wonderful salads – lettuces, tomatoes, spring onions, watercress from the same stream in which we sometimes lost our cricket-balls – and generally a ham, home-smoked at the Adam and Eve and decorated with paper frills and parsley so that it looked like a picture out of Mrs Beeton. The tea interval was always a long one at Brensham.

And now the captains have tossed and Sammy Hunt leads us out to field. Sammy has a completely bald head, which at the beginning of the season appears startlingly white; but he scorns to wear a hat, and as the season progresses his pate becomes rubicund, and then gradually goes brown, until by mid-August it is the colour of an over-wintered russet apple. Mr Chorlton, of course, wears his harlequin cap, the gayest cap in cricket, but it's old and faded and it's the very same cap, he tells us, in which he ran about the field for hours, in 1895, chasing the ball which Archie Maclaren hit so mercilessly when he scored 424 against Somerset. Mr Mountjoy, who wears his I. Zingari cap, must have been a useful cricketer too in his young days; but he can't run very fast or bend very quickly, and his old eyes – so sharp at spotting the chiff-chaff in the willow tree – are too slow to follow the ball which comes quick off the pitch and breaks away. Therefore his innings generally end with a loud *snick* and a yell of 'How's that?' from the delighted wicket-keeper; and as the umpire's finger goes up Mr Mountjoy mutters sadly: 'Oh Lord, that awful noise again!'

Sammy begins to arrange his field, doing so with humanity and a sense of the fitness of things. Thus Mr Mountjoy, since he can't run far, goes to mid-off and to save him walking between overs takes point when the bowling is from the other end. Mr Chorlton, who can't or won't run at all, keeps wicket; and another elderly member of the team, a retired engineer called Hope-Kingley, alternates between mid-on and square-leg. But Briggs the blacksmith, who has huge horny hands with which he sometimes bends a six-inch nail for fun, must stand at forward short-leg or in the deep, and take what's coming to him; the village policeman goes in the slips, because, says Sammy, that's a suitable place for a bobby – 'they catch you out when you're not looking.' Billy Butcher, who is the village ne'er-do-weel and drunkard, is sent to long-leg in the hope that a bit of running about will do him good; and the 'boys', a collective term for any youths whom the Secretary has roped in at the last moment to make up the team, are distributed round the boundary where with luck some high hits will harden up their palms. As for Sammy himself, he will be anywhere and everywhere, wherever the catches come low and hard, wherever the new red ball races towards the boundary there will by Sammy's bald head bobbing after it; for he is like a good general who turns up unexpectedly wherever the fight is hottest.

Our Secretary, a small, wiry market-gardener called Alfie, takes the ball for the first over. Joe Trentfield, our umpire and the landlord of the Horse Narrow, counts his six pennies and drops them one by one into the pocket of his smock. Dai Roberts the postman opens his score book at the pavilion window and licks the point of his pencil.

'Play!' says Joe: and the season begins.

The Captain

Sailors hardly ever take to cricket; they don't get the chance to practise, for one thing, and for another, I think cricket is a game for people who have roots, it is a territorial game, in which men really do bowl and bat with greater satisfaction when they do so for the place they belong to. It is an expression of parochialism; and even the County sides, which play for the money, would scorn to buy and sell their players as footballers do, dealing in men as stockbrokers deal in shares. Thus if you should meet, say, the Lancashire side and the Gloucestershire side together in a pub you could easily differentiate them by their accents; and when Somerset and Yorkshire go on tour they take the speech of Somerset and Yorkshire with them. This territorial aspect of the game is even more evident in village cricket; and people were sometimes quite shocked that I should be allowed to play for Brensham, although I lived only four miles away. Peripatetic cricketers, who hawk their batsmanship or their fast bowling round all the teams in the district and change sides as often as Warwick the King-Maker are rare and generally disapproved of; certainly Brensham would have nothing to do with them. For cricket, as I have said, is somehow mixed up with our vigorous parochialism; and when Brensham goes out to field on Saturday afternoon, it is Brensham going to war.

Therefore it was curious that Sammy Hunt should be our captain; for he was one of the rootless, heartless ones, a sailor, and hadn't had the opportunity, during his wandering life, to learn that absurd loyalty to a piece of well-kept turf. It was curious of course, that he should have settled down at Brensham at all, to 'muck about with little boats', as he put it, 'on a piddling little river'. I suppose all sailors carry with them about the world, in addition to that small green kit-bag of their personal possessions, a dream of green fields; and for most of them the dream fades or the salt water tarnishes it; but somehow or other Sammy managed to keep his fresh and bright so that when the time came for him to retire he knew exactly what kind of a cottage he wanted, knew all about the green-sprouting osiers and the slow winding river, bent like a bow as it runs round the hill, and the water-meadows where in June the wind-waves trouble the mowing-grass as if it were the sea.

However, Sammy never forgot that he was a sailor; and he often enlivened the cricket-matches with great sea-oaths or astonished the opposing team by shouting to his bowler: 'Pitch the beggar one on the starboard side!' or commanding

a fieldman to 'move round a couple of points to port'.
In the pub afterwards he would sooner or later launch
himself into one of his long salty tales, about how he ran out
of coal during a storm in the Bay of Biscay, or how he dealt
with a mutiny at Tiensin, or how he nearly married a geisha
girl in Japan; but although we knew these tales so well, and
loved to hear Sammy telling them, we never learned what
happened in the end: closing-time always came too soon,
leaving Sammy's tramp-steamer drifting helplessly towards
Vigo, Sammy driving the mutineers into the fo'c'sle with
his bare fists, or Sammy and his geisha girl locked in a
timeless embrace on the seafront of Yokohama.

The Secretary

On the cricket-field Sammy's word was law; but between
matches it was Alfie Perks, the Secretary, who held the team
together, who saw to the buying of the bats, balls, pads,
gloves, stumps and score-books we needed, and who organized the dreadful rummage sale which was supposed to wipe
out the usual autumnal deficit and the whist drive and
dance which actually did so when the rummage sale had
failed. It was he who wrote, painfully, slowly, and rather
illiterately, those long complicated letters to other Secretar-
ies, and made sense of their complicated and illiterate
replies, so that by mid-February, when the pitch generally
lay two feet under water and cricket seemed further off
than the Millennium, he was able to send to the printer our
list of fixtures for the next season. When the season came
round, it was Alfie who had the job of notifying the players –
eleven postcards scratched out in agonized copper-plate! –
of arranging the transport – Who had a car? Who had a
motor-bike? Who had room for a fat man with a cricket

bag? – and of drawing the pub at midday on Saturday for those very uncertain quantities, 'the boys', who were always likely to let us down because they were haymaking or harvesting, or wanted to go fishing or to dig in their gardens or to fiddle with their motor-bikes or to take their wenches to the pictures.

All this would have been extremely burdensome if Alfie had allowed it to worry him; but being a market-gardener and fruit-grower, owning twelve acres of plum orchard and five of apple, his fortune hanging yearly on the chancy weather between April and June, he had long ago given up worrying about anything. He knew that a soft spring might make him prosperous, a late frost might ruin him. There was nothing he could do about it, except grin and bear it; so Alfie grinned. His grin was characteristic, typical, and familiar. With it he greeted impartially the sight of overladen boughs in good seasons or blackened buds after frost. Fruit-growing, he said, was like horse-racing; but there were more certainties on the racecourse. If he lost all his fruit, or if Mr Chorlton dropped three catches running off his bowling, Alfie grinned and shrugged his shoulders; and his comment on the large disaster was the same as his summary of the little one: That's the way it is.

Alfie bowled leg-breaks: three paces to the wicket, longish fair hair falling over his forehead, a hop, skip and a jump, and an innocent-looking good-length ball delivered with a sort of tousled grin. He was one of those small persistent men who inevitably remind one of terriers; and as it happened he owned a small tousled terrier, which also grinned. It was called Rexy and it followed Alfie everywhere and somehow resembled him; for both had bushy eyebrows, an air of perky truculence, and a humorous acceptance of fate. For a week or two in late winter the resemblance was even closer. Alfie's face, at that season, went brick-red and peeled as if he'd been in the sun, although there had been no strong sun for months. His eyebrows and eyelashes became curiously sandy, like those of desert soldiers. Rexy's eyebrows, nose and whiskers went sandy too, and when we saw him running about the village like that we knew that Alfie had been spraying.

For the spray dripped off the trees into the grass and stained Rexy's paws as he followed his master. Whenever there was a wind the liquid blew back like fine rain into Alfie's face and burned it, peeled his nose and bleached his eyebrows, and made his eyes as red as a ferret's. Both master and dog looked as if they had just come back from crossing the Sahara.

This tedious uncomfortable business of spraying was probably the biggest single operation in Alfie's busy year. It took a long time, and it was also very expensive; so that less conscientious growers were apt to 'give it a miss' in seasons when their bank balances were in red or when they wanted to buy a new motor-car. There was a great temptation to do so; for if a sharp frost should come when the fruit was just forming, all the money and labour of spraying would have been spent in vain. The frost could slay more plums in a night than the little green caterpillars could devour in a season; and as the fruit-growers said when they looked for an excuse: 'You can't spray against Jack Frost.'

But Alfie, who was painstaking and persistent and whose integrity showed itself in everything he did, never made that excuse. He felt, I think, a sort of obligation to his trees. He must do his best for them; and if thereafter the frost took all, if there was not a plum left on the boughs nor a penny of profit from all the twelve acres, he would still have the curious consolation that his orchards looked 'clean', the abhorred caterpillars did not thrive in them, his neighbours need have no fear lest the pest should spread from Alfie's land. He had the true countryman's dislike of a botched job, the craftsman's determination to leave nothing to chance. So every year, in January or February, Rexy went blond as a film star and Alfie with his peeling face looked very unlike a film star indeed, and the village knew that Alfie was spraying. Once again he'd decided to put off buying a motor-car.

This, I think, is how I shall always remember him: with a grin on his red, raw face and his eyebrows and eyelashes ginger-blond, and ginger-blond too the lock of hair which always pokes out from under his cap: with ginger-pawed Rexy sardonically grinning at his heels; walking among the trees which bear proud names like Blenheim and Victoria, looking up into the dripping boughs and then glancing at the inscrutable sky and shrugging his shoulders as an old gambler does while he watches the desperate race, his fancy lying third, and still a hundred yards to go.

The Blacksmith

Jeremy Briggs, who helped Mr Chorlton to make our pitch one of the best in the West Country, was another craftsman. At his blacksmith's forge, when he was not shoeing horses, he would contrive you almost anything from a cigarette-lighter to a set of fire-irons or a pair of wrought-iron gates. On the cricket-field he lumbered about rather like one of those great slow farm-horses whose enormous hairy hoofs he cared for. Between matches he often mowed the ground for us, or patiently dragged the heavy roller to and fro, to and fro between the creases while Mr Chorlton with a pocket-knife dug up the daisies, and filled in the holes. These two, as they worked together, carried on an argument which never ended; for Briggs was a Socialist and Mr Chorlton, whose wide classical reading had persuaded him that the political troubles of Athens and Rome were much the same as ours, believed that mankind was incapable of improvement and that no doctrine could save it from damnation. The argument continued from week to week and was abandoned in September only to be resumed in the following April. When Briggs' rolling took him down the pitch away from the crease where Mr Chorlton knelt before a daisy, Briggs began to shout; and Mr Chorlton shouted back, so that you could hear them in Magpie Lane, the one quoting Marx, the other Pericles. Our nearly-perfect cricket-pitch was really a by-product of their differences; for if they hadn't enjoyed arguing we should not have had two good groundsmen for nothing.

Briggs' smithy was next door to the Adam and Eve. There was no spreading chestnut tree, only a heap of old iron in the yard, with some broken carts, rusty farm implements and dismantled motor-cars. A notice-board announced: 'J. BRIGGS, SHOEING ETC. SMITH. CONTRACTS UNDERTOOK. ODD-JOBING.' I once asked him what Contracts he Undertook; and it turned out that he had an arrangement with a market-gardener to shoe his pony all round twice a year in return for four bundles of asparagus and a pot of plums.

There was plenty of work for Briggs in Brensham. Most of the farmers' sons had their hunters and Point-to-Pointers, the district abounded with children's ponies, there was a riding-school at Elmbury, and the Hunt stables were only five miles away. Briggs, for whom the colour red had a very different connotation from that of pink coats, shod these Hunt horses somewhat reluctantly, pointing out to the Whips and Second Horsemen who brought them to his smithy that Hunt Servants were merely the misguided flunkeys of the idle rich. The Whips, secure in their certainty that jumping a stiff blackthorn or hollering a fox away as he crept

down the winter covertside was a very different thing from
flunkeydom, merely smiled and wondered how a man who
could handle horses so confidently came to believe in
Labour. There was a close association, in their minds,
between horseflesh and Conservatism.

But when it came to a question of working for the Syndicate Briggs stuck his toes in. The Syndicate kept horses for
hacking; they did not hunt. They liked, we thought, to have
their photographs taken on horseback when they came
down from town for the weekend. Briggs, who merely
disapproved of the Hunt, really hated the Syndicate. The
Hunt, after all, performed its wicked Capitalist actions
openly, publicly and indeed ostentatiously, with shiny top-
hats and red coats and polished top-boots. It galloped over
your holding and broke down your fences with a hurrah
and a holloa. If you got in the way, and General Bouverie
cursed you, you could curse him back; you could scowl at the
elegant gentlemen and the great ladies and the fat smug farmers and the feckless farmers' sons and pleasantly contem-
plate stringing them up to the lamp-posts in the fullness of
time. But the Syndicate worked in darkness and in disguise:
it was the kind of Capitalism which pulled the invisible
wires and made poor men dance to its tune. It was part of
the monstrous mysterious Thing which sent up the rent of
cottages and sent down the miner's wage; which contrived
a glut of coffee in Brazil or a rice famine in Bengal by fidd-
ling about in some unexplained way with Foreign Exchange.
In some unspecified fashion, Briggs was sure of it, the
Syndicate was associated with the terrible, powerful, name-
less people whom he thought of as 'They'. 'They' had their
offices in London and New York and Amsterdam; 'They'
were supernatural; 'They' played with Governments as if
Governments were pawns, stood above Prime Ministers and
Kings, and laughed cynically at revolutions, being confident

that 'They' could easily corrupt the revolutionaries with the gift of a little illusory power. 'They' was invisible, anonymous, unidentified; you couldn't curse them, break their windows, imprison them or hang them. Briggs had serious doubts whether even the Russian Communists had effectively got rid of Them.

Seeing in the Syndicate's workings a trivial, fragmentary manifestation of Their power, Briggs stoutly refused to shoe their horses and assaulted their Head Groom who apparently 'called him names'. For this he was bound over by the Justices of the Peace for Elmbury. 'What did he actually call you?' asked General Bouverie, who was Chairman of the Bench.

'A bloody Bolshie, your Worship,' said Briggs.

'Very provocative. I should have hit him myself,' said General Bouverie, who knew all about Briggs' politics. 'In the circumstances I shall refrain from imposing a fine.'

Of course, Briggs could easily afford to refuse the custom of the Syndicate; he was an extremely prosperous tradesman. There is a mistaken notion that the blacksmith's is a dying trade; and those who are always moaning and mourning the departure of Ye Olde things, the William-Morrissy-arty-crafty people, will tell you that the village smith is disappearing, another craftsman-victim of 'the thing we miscall Progress'. In fact I believe that Jeremy Briggs made a good deal more money than James Briggs his father, who owned the smithy before him. It is true that there were not so many farm-horses in 1930 as there were in late Victorian times (although there were more hunters); but the 'odd-jobbing' which he so proudly advertised more than re-dressed the balance. If there were fewer horses, there was more farm-machinery; and when the binder or the hay-sweep went wrong it was generally the blacksmith's job to put it right. Again, fewer horses meant more motor-cars;

and these motor-cars from time to time ran into each other head-on. When the drivers had been taken to hospital, and the vehicles had been towed to the garage, and the doctors, the motor-manufacturers and the garagemen had all levied their dues upon the insurance company, there often remained a kind of residue in the shape of two bent front-axles which found their way to Briggs' forge. Besides, being a skilled worker in most metals, Briggs made a good many profitable odds-and-ends in his spare time; the local builder alone gave him enough work to pay for the beer which he drank in enormous quantities. He certainly didn't deserve the pity of the arty-crafty crowd who went in for folk-dancing and played upon pan-pipes and taught long-suffering villagers to make useless things out of raffia.

Like most blacksmiths, Briggs possessed notable biceps, forearms and hands. When he was a young man he could tear a pack of cards in two. His palms were criss-crossed with old calloused scars, which were the consequence of his youthful foolishness in bending six-inch nails for the entertainment of the company at the Adam and Eve. In later years, becoming less reckless, he wrapped handkerchiefs round his hand before starting his demonstration.

At one time he was the terror of travelling showmen at the local fairs; for whether it was a matter of bending pokers or lifting weights, Briggs could always do it better than they could. When the Strongest Man in the World with painful effort and streams of perspiration had managed to give a slight twist to an iron bar, Briggs, pleading with affected innocence 'Let me try that, mister! Let me have a go!' would mount the rostrum and without apparent exertion bend the bar almost double. All the Strongest Men in the World hated and feared him.

At Elmbury Mop he elected one night to try his strength upon one of those machines which you smite with a mallet.

He had had a great deal of beer, and what happened would have served as a good advertisement for the brewery. With his first shot, being as he freely admitted a bit unsteady on his pins, he missed altogether. The showman laughed; and this annoyed him. He took a lot of trouble over his next shot, his great hands which had clamped in their awful grip the kicking hoof of an angry stallion clasped the handle of the mallet, the muscles of his forearms stood out like the roots of an old tree, and Briggs smote. He hit the machine fair and square with such force that it fell apart; the head of the mallet flew off into the crowd. Satisfied, he shrugged his shoulders and walked away.

Yet at cricket he hardly ever hit sixes, but batted with a huge stolidity which would have done credit to a Lancashire stone-waller; his favourite stroke was what he imagined to be a neat and professional cut through the slips, off which he was generally caught in the gulley. And at darts he had a most curious style which seemed to be a flat contradiction of his great size and strength: he threw rather like a girl. He possessed a set of darts of his own, very tiny and, as one might say, sissy darts, which he picked up deliberately between his enormous fingers (which weren't half as clumsy as they looked) and propelled very neatly and primly into the particular double or treble he wanted.

The Potterer

At the time when I began to play cricket for Brensham, the elderly, sick-looking, sallow-faced man called Hope-Kingley was a newcomer there; and the village didn't quite know what to make of him. He was shy and extremely reserved; and he never talked about himself. He had a quiet, pleasant, middle-aged wife and one small son. We knew he had lived abroad for most of his life, but that was all. Jeremy Briggs said he was a very good example of the Idle Rich who had nothing better to do than potter about; and although there was no evidence that he was rich we all agreed that he was a Potterer. He started pottering as soon as he was settled in his house. He began to build himself a rock-garden, and left it half-done to make a lily-pond. He went in for Aquaria. He bred Sealyhams. He planted expensive Alpines in the unfinished rock-garden, and the slugs devoured them. He tried without much success to grow asparagus and prize sweet-peas.

He seemed to do nothing very well. You would meet him wandering about with a gun under his arm and he would tell you that he was Pottering after Pigeons; but it was very rarely that he shot anything and when he did so he was generally more embarrassed than pleased. I once saw him haloed as it were with a cloud of pale grey feathers, blood spattered all over his face, and a pigeon's head in one hand, its body in the other. 'I wounded it,' he confessed miserably, 'and I didn't know how to kill it. I wanted to put the poor thing out of its misery, so I tried to screw its neck; and then as you see I panicked.'

Encouraged by Mr Chorlton, he even took to butterfly-collecting; but he wasn't very good at that either. I have stood and watched him chasing Clouded Yellows, which are as fleet as Atalanta, among the tall thistles at the edge of a field of lucerne, and he has reminded me, as he pranced about, of a rather battered and elderly faun. I confess I laughed; and of course he didn't catch any Clouded Yellows. In the end he had to employ Johnnie Perks, Alfie's son, who got him half a dozen in ten minutes.

Children loved him. They didn't seem to notice his tiresome ineffectiveness. Although he wore thick glasses and had rather bleary eyes it seemed that he was able to find birds'-

nests which even schoolboys failed to find; and during the nesting season you hardly ever saw him without three or four of the village brats at his heels. One day we heard that he had actually shinned up a tree, in search of a magpie's nest, and had become stuck there. Magpies generally build in the thickest and thorniest of trees and poor old Hope-Kingley hung there like Absalom. The attendant children rescued him, of course, and the incident merely strengthened their conviction that he was some kind of hero. For our part we remarked that the old boy must be getting into his second childhood; and Jeremy Briggs said it would have served him right if he'd broken his neck.

At cricket, as at everything else, he simply pottered. He bowled a bit and batted a bit (though he was extremely liable to run out himself or his fellow batsman) and he fielded with sublime ineptitude for though he was incapable of catching or picking up the ball himself he frequently contrived to collide with anybody else who was about to do so. If he did get hold of the ball he threw it in with great force several yards wide of the wicket-keeper, so that it went to the boundary.

However, he apologized so nicely for all his mistakes, and seemed to enjoy the game so much, that Sammy hadn't the heart to drop him from the team. In any case we were generally two players short by noon on Saturday and would have gladly fielded a blind man if he'd offered to turn out for us.

One summer – it must have been Hope-Kingley's second at Brensham – the old potterer tired of his rock-garden, his lily-pond, his Sealyhams, his goldfish and his butterflies and determined to dam the stream which ran through his orchard and to make a big pool which he could stock with rainbow trout. He undertook this task himself, and would accept no advice or assistance from anybody. He carried it out, so it seemed to us, in a very slipshod and amateurish way, and we warned him that his dam wouldn't hold, the water would run out of it. 'Dear, dear!' he said. 'Perhaps it will. How foolish I am!' And sure enough, he let the water in that night, and the new pond was dry again by breakfast-time. Briggs, who had prophesied this, spent most of his dinner-hour leaning on the orchard gate and grinning at the muddy morass. Other villagers, more polite, told Mr Hope-Kingley:

'We're very sorry to hear about your trout-pond!'
The old man smiled a queer and quizzical smile.
'Dear me,' he said. 'I shall have to try again.'

Once more he let in the water; and once more the pond was dry within twelve hours. And again, when people sympathized, Mr Hope-Kingley gave them that queer little smile.

The next day, as it happened, was the King's birthday, and the honours came out in the paper. Somebody, glancing through the list of 'Knights', read with astonishment:

> *'To be Knight Commander of the Indian Empire: Gerald Devereux Hope-Kingley: For distinguished services in hydraulic engineering in India, Burma and Malay.'*

Mr Chorlton and I were not altogether surprised, when we passed the trout-pond that evening on our way to fish in the river, to find that it was full; and this time the water was not running out. Hope-Kingley was pottering in his garden.

'Sir Gerald,' said Mr Chorlton. 'You've been pulling our legs.'

'Dear me,' he said mildly. 'You must forgive me. You must let an old man have his little joke.'

He asked us in to have a glass of sherry. He showed us the

rock-garden and the slug-bitten Alpines, and his draggled collection of butterflies and the tropical fishes in his aquarium which were dying off from some mysterious disease.

'You see,' he said, 'none of these things go right, do they? And I suppose that's because I'm such an awful potterer. For forty years I promised myself, almost every day, that when I retired I would give myself the pleasure of deciding over my early-morning tea what particular form of pottering I should practise after breakfast!'

I thought of the long uncomfortable years that had given him the right to potter: the steamy jungles of Burma and Malay, the high peaks of the North-west Frontier, the great watersheds above Nepal; the malaria and the insects and the damp heat which blurred the eyepiece of the theodolite; the great rains and the melting snow and the rivers thundering down and the agony of waiting to see whether the dam would hold.

Sir Gerald butted in upon my thoughts.

'Next autumn,' he said, 'I'm going to make a bird-table outside my study window. And then I shall rig up some sort of camera contrivance so that I can photograph the birds. One might invent an automatic one, don't you think, which would take a picture whenever a bird alighted on the table? It would amuse me when I'm kept to the house, which is pretty often; for I had too long in the tropics to stick an English winter well. I always promised myself that when I couldn't even potter I'd amuse myself with a bird-table and rig up a camera to photograph the birds.'

The 'Boys'

The last five or six places in our cricket-team were filled, generally at the last moment, by various unreliable and often unwilling youths whom Alfie impressed out of the pubs: labouring boys, farmers' sons, and so on. The former, who toiled all the week in the fields and market-gardens, found no enjoyment whatever in chasing a cricket-ball in the hot sun upon their afternoon off; the latter, whose interest lay chiefly in fiery horses and powerful motor-bikes, had little enthusiasm for a game which offered no prospect of a broken neck. However, Alfie by his press-gang methods usually captured a few of them; and some, especially the farmers' sons, often slogged happily and heartily or took a few wickets with their murderous fast bowling.

We included in the category of 'the boys', because they were equally unreliable, Billy Butcher the village ne'er-do-weel and Banks, the village policeman. We could not count on either: the former because he was almost always drunk and the latter because he was often on duty. On one occasion we lost both players through the same cause: Billy Butcher chose a Saturday afternoon to go roaring round the village merrily breaking windows, and Banks was called out to arrest him.

That must have been the only arrest Banks made in his first five years at Brensham. He arrived, as all our village policemen do, as a young, efficient and rather officious constable, eager for promotion, willing to go out of his way to look for trouble, and inclined to hang about in the neighbourhood of the pubs at closing-time. He had succeeded an elderly, easy-going fellow who knew our ways; and at first we regarded Banks with suspicion and dismay. But Joe Trentfield, the landlord of the Horse Narrow, who'd seen village policemen come and go for twenty years, laughed at our fears and said philosophically: ' 'Tis allus the same with new brooms. Wait a bit, and you'll see we'll tame him. Be they real tigers, Brensham allus tames 'em in the end.'

And sure enough, we tamed Banks. We married him off, for one thing, to Joe Trentfield's daughter. We persuaded him to play for us at cricket and darts. Sam Hunt built him a boat and taught him to fish for chub. Soon he learned that the business of a village constable was concerned, not with criminals and crooks, but with foot and mouth disease and swine fever, straying animals and lost dogs: and that the nearest he was likely to get to dealing with a murder was his annual duty of quelling a row between the Fitchers and the Gormleys about a murder which had happened fifty years ago. He discovered (Joe Trentfield's daughter may have had something to do with the discovery) that the best way of making sure that the pub closed at ten was to drop in for a quiet drink with the landlord at ten-thirty. He found out that prosecuting people for having no dog licence or riding a bicycle without lights was not, after all, a short cut to promotion; and before very long the dream of quick promotion faded, and a different dream took its place: he began to save up towards buying a cottage with perhaps a little orchard and a couple of pigstyes, so that he could still live in the shadow of Brensham Hill when he retired.

The Drunkard

Billy Butcher, at the age of thirty-five, was still the village's Problem Child. He was incorrigible and anti-social and I suppose that in the sort of society advocated by Mr Bernard Shaw he would have been told 'We bear you no ill will, my dear fellow, but society must be protected' and popped into a humane and hygienic lethal chamber in no time. We, on the other hand, having a vague and unformulated belief that one of the fundamental Rights of Man was his right to go to the devil in his own fashion, bought him drinks, lent him money, put up with his occasional bouts of window-smashing, and in fact allowed him to drink himself slowly towards a far more uncomfortable death than Mr Shaw would have devised for him.

Was society worse off in consequence, or better? I don't know. We should have been richer by more than a few pounds; for Billy was an expensive companion. But what are a few pounds compared with a lot of laughter, a lot of low comedy, a fragment of high comedy, an hour or two every week of wild and gorgeous talk? Billy gave us all that; for he was two other things as well as a drunkard, things which do not often go together: he was a clown and he was a poet. His clowning was spontaneous, irrepressible, and sometimes sublime. He didn't have to try to be funny, and his fooling was of the same nature as Sir Andrew Aguecheek's, it 'came natural'. The truth of the matter was, I think, that for certain brief periods in the process of his drunkenness he saw the whole of life as an absurd and enormous comedy, and all he did then was to play his own part in it. If he made us laugh, it was simply because we, to him, appeared almost unbearably funny. Finding the whole world peopled with figures of fun, he did no more than adapt himself to his environment.

As for his poetry, that was a very different matter. It was not at all obvious, it was something which had its source deep within him, it dwelt in the secret places of Billy's heart where no doubt it teased and tortured and tormented him as such Daemons will. To quell it he drank whisky: more and more whisky, have another boys, well I don't mind if I do, down the hatch – and perhaps if he drank long enough the Daemon lay still. But sometimes the opposite thing happened. There was a Tom Tiddler's Ground, a no-man's-land between semi-drunkenness and complete drunkenness, in which shadowy territory Billy sometimes found himself. Then for an hour, or half an hour, the poetry would bubble up. He became possessed. He talked sublime and airy nonsense. He quoted. His subconscious heaved – and brought up great undigested slabs of Shakespeare, gobbets of Swinburne, ill-assorted scraps and fragments from Chaucer, Skelton, Sir Thomas Browne. He was not showing off; it was sheer agony: the stuff gushed out of him. But the fit didn't last long. Let's have another, he cried almost desperately, another and another, as if the whisky were a sort of purge for poetry: and soon he was empty. Then we would see the sweat standing out on his forehead and the tears welling up in his eyes. 'I can't bear it,' Billy would say.

'Bear what?'

'Everything.'

And then, leaning against the bar, with his head in his hands, he would cry his heart out, until some kindly person led him away.

If Billy had been a newcomer, I suppose we should have been less tolerant of him; but he was a native of Brensham, born in the pleasant house called Gables which Hope-Kingley now owned. He was the son of Colonel Butcher, a stiff moustachio'd warrior-scholar who had spent his last ten years in our village writing a grammar of the Urdu language. His wife had died in India, and the boy ran wild as a Brensham hare. While the old gentleman worked in his study, young Billy at the age of seventeen was discovering the queer dirty little pubs in the back streets of Elmbury and flirting with alley-wenches at Elmbury Mop. There was some trouble, when Billy was eighteen, over a girl in the village; and Colonel Butcher briefly interrupted his study of Urdu to deal with the situation, which he did by packing Billy off to a crammer for the Army. Six months later the boy was back; no princely fee, said the crammer, would compensate him for the disgrace and ill-fame which Billy's

presence brought upon his establishment. So the Urdu
grammar suffered another set-back while its author made
arrangements to dispatch his son to West Africa. 'At least,'
he said bitterly, 'you will find no blonde housemaids there.'
This was doubtless true; but Billy found something much
more dangerous. When his father, having completed the
grammar, died of boredom and old age, Billy came back to
Brensham and we knew at once that the whisky held him
in its power as no woman could ever do. We could see him
hurrying down to the Trumpet or the Adam and Eve at a
quarter to ten in the morning, in order to be there exactly at
opening-time; we would watch how his hand shook as he
lifted the first glass, how it became curiously steady after the
third; we would notice the bulge in his pocket as he tottered
home after closing-time. A few well-meaning people tried
to help him: but most of us knew that it was already too
late and we accepted Billy for what he was: a hopeless,
incurable, incorrigible drunkard. His father had left him a
good deal of money, and he spent it in a few years. Then he
sold the house, and the library, and the furniture, and took
a room above Mrs Doan's shop. Then he sold his car and
bought a motor-bike; sold the motor-bike; borrowed from
moneylenders; and in his last extremity borrowed from his
friends. At this juncture, when everybody was saying that he
had come to the end of his tether, he received a lucky wind-
fall: an uncle died and left him some money but, knowing
Billy, appointed two trustees to prevent him from squander-
ing it. These hard-hearted men (as Billy described them to
us) doled him out the sum of three pounds a week and
by dint of borrowing, sponging, and forgetting to pay Mrs
Doan (who adored him) he contrived to keep himself
headed for a toper's grave, though of necessity his pace
towards it became slower. In the fruit season he hired
himself out, for he had no silly pride, to the farmers for

plum-picking and cherry-picking. On one hot July day, being extremely drunk, he fell off a twenty-rung ladder on to his head. A sober man would have broken his neck; but the only effect it had on Billy was to make him slightly more lachrymose after his outbursts of poetry and slightly less controllable when the whim took him to break people's windows.

The Scorer

Brensham possessed another poet; but this one was serious and sober, shared none of our easy-going ways, was alien in speech and spirit, and had brought with him across the border the dark and twisted puritanism of the dark valleys. He was the postman; as he called himself, Dai Roberts Postman, using his function as a surname in the Welsh fashion. He had come holidaying out of some black village in the spring of 1919, when miners had money to spend, and had fallen in love with our green hill and our snowy orchards and with one of our pink, plump village girls, so he never went back. I think he fell in love with the Syndicate's pheasants also; he was a better poacher than a postman. However, he insisted that his true calling was neither of these: he was a poet. Long ago, in his bleak black valley, in the slate-roofed horrible Hall next to the tin bethel, an Eisteddfod had taken place; and Dai had recited a long poem before the minor bards on the theme of Sodom and Gomorrah, which had frightened them into giving him the prize. Since then he had rested upon his laurels, though he once told us that he was contemplating an epic, longer than the Mabinogion, upon the subject of The Approaching End of the World. But the great project hung fire. In our flowery countryside there were no Eisteddfodau: we indulged in

profane pastimes, cricket on the village green, darts
matches in the pub, dances in the village hall. The flesh-
pots corrupted us, said Dai; and true poetry blossomed
only in the cold slatey valleys and in the hearts of the small
dark singing men.

Dai never entered any of the pubs; to do so, he believed,
meant certain damnation. Nor would he ever take his plump,
cheerful wife to the whist drives and dances which enlivened
the winter evenings for so many of the villagers; a Baptist
Minister had assured him long ago that a girl who went to
dances was a sister of the Devil, and he still believed this.
On Saturday afternoons, however, he was willing to watch
our cricket-matches, and although he did not play the game
he generously admitted that 'he could see no great harm in
it, upon a week-day'. Before long he was persuaded to score
for us; and as the seasons went by the casual job became a
permanent and official one, so that we took Dai with us
when we played away matches and he 'followed' Brensham
as the ardent spectators of football 'follow' the Arsenal or
the Spurs. He kept our batting and bowling averages from
match to match throughout the season, and did not forget
to tell us if they were unsatisfactory. 'One hundred and
sixty runs your bowling has cost,' he would chant, 'for only
four wick-ets! That iss an average of fifty-three point three
recurring!' Indeed in his eagerness that Brensham should
win he became sharply critical of all the players. 'Mr Moore,'
he told me, after I had most painfully missed a high catch in
the deep, 'you will not mind me saying that you would
catch the ball better if you did not first let it bounce off
your breastbone.' Of Mr Mountjoy, whom he held to be
idolatrous, he declared: 'He flicks at the ball as if he were
sprinkling it with holy wat-er!' He disapproved of Mr
Chorlton's harlequin cap (which provoked him, apparently,
in the same inexplicable way as Douglas Jardine's provoked

the Australians), of Sammy's bald head – 'A sunstroke he does deserve for being so fool-ish!' – of the placing of the field, the choice of the bowlers, and the batting order. It was a wonder that he could bring himself to score for us at all, since our antics drove him into such despair. In any case the duties of scorer are dull and exacting. We asked him, one day, what pleasure he got out of it.

'Like a sonnet the well-kept score-sheet iss,' was his astonishing answer.

The Helpers

As I have said, we were proud of our cricket-teas and of the pretty girls who served them. Alfie used both as bait for 'the boys' when he was trying to make up the team at the last moment. 'Sally Doan will be there,' he'd remark casually. Sally had honey-blonde hair and soft brown eyes and a side-ways look for any respectable youth. Or to the older, the more sedate, and the married men, Alfie would say: 'They tell me we're going to cut a two-year-old ham, the best they've ever cured at the Adam and Eve.' By such stratagems we managed to field a complete team at almost every home match throughout the season.

Mrs Hartley, the landlord's wife from the Adam and Eve, was the organizing genius of the Helpers. It was she who provided the hams, the salads, the meat-pies, the home-made pickles at the very small cost of one and threepence a head. She was a plump good-looking bustling girl whose chief delight in life seemed to be providing huge meals for other people. Her husband, a comparatively slight fellow when he married her, now turned the scale at sixteen stone. Great sides of bacon, hams weighing twenty-five pounds apiece, hung from the ceiling of her immaculate store-room; and upon a score of long shelves were rows of jam-jars, bottling-jars, pickle-jars, all neatly labelled in her round hand: Piccalilli 1921, Black B. and Apple, Pickled Walnuts, cucumbers and so on. There were great quantities of home-made wine as well, likewise labelled: Sloe Gin 1917, Elder-flower 1919, Parsnip 1920, Dandelion May 1921 – as if these were the proud titles of famous vintages, which indeed for the inhabitants of Brensham they were.

To assist her with the sandwich-cutting, the pouring out, and so on, Mrs Hartley had roped in, as well as Sally Doan, the two youngest daughters of Joe Trentfield of the Horse Narrow. (The eldest was already married to Constable Banks and must mind the police station when he was playing cricket.) At the time I am writing of they were aged fifteen and seventeen and they were already as flirtatious a pair of little hussies as you could possibly imagine. Their names were Mimi and Meg. They both had corn-coloured hair, blue eyes, rather snub noses, pink cheeks, high breasts, and irrepressible giggles. When I first saw them together I was troubled with an old memory; I knew it was something to do with my childhood, and yet I could not define what it was. Dolls, perhaps? But it wasn't dolls; the flesh-and-blood was too palpable in Mimi and Meg. Suddenly I had it. The chorus at the Pantomime! The first pantomime I ever saw; and a row of little girls who appeared, to me, to be astonishingly naked, with pink faces and big eyes, prancing down the stage and kicking their legs in the air and singing in tinny voices:

'Hell-lo every-body! Hell-lo every-body!'

and then, a moment later:

'We are the Fairies, dancing on the Green,
But hush! Who comes? . . . It is the Fairy Queen!'

My heart had sunk at that; I was not at all interested in the Fairy Queen or in the little pink-cheeked girls with their pink tights which were somehow more fleshy than flesh; I wanted to see the conjurer. But the memory stuck, and when I met Mimi and Meg it popped out of the mysterious attic in which all such junk is stored.

Then a remarkable thing happened. One November afternoon, coming back from hunting, I called at the Horse Narrow for a drink. It was long before opening-time but in Brensham that didn't matter; I tethered my horse in the back-yard and went into the living room. There was an unusual air of bustle and excitement. Fat Mrs Trentfield, whose enormous bosom bounced whenever she moved – would the girls look like that thirty years hence? – was brushing Meg's hair. Mimi, in front of the looking-glass, was simultaneously powdering her nose and practising the steps of a mincing dance. Joe Trentfield was coming downstairs with two large suitcases. 'Excuse the mess,' said Mrs Trentfield, 'but the girls are just off.'

'Off?'

'Why, didn't you know? They're going to Birmingham, to act in the Pantomime.'

Mimi said:

'We had an audition. The producer was ever so nice.'

'Ever so,' echoed Meg. 'He's put us in the chorus.'

''Twill turn their heads,' said Joe, sombrely but not without pride.

'Sing Mr Moore that song you've been practising,' said Mrs Trentfield. 'It's ever so nice.'

Meg sat at the piano. Mimi stood beside her. I waited hopefully, half-expecting to hear 'Hello, Everybody'; but it was a trivial tinkling song about Thinking of you When skies are blue. It was terrible, and Mimi sang it terribly.

'Pretty, isn't it?' said Mrs Trentfield. 'But sad.'

Then the taxi arrived. The girls rushed upstairs to see if they'd left anything behind. Mrs Trentfield bustled and bounced. Joe pronounced unheeded valedictory warnings against Young Men. Squeaking with excitement, the girls came scampering downstairs. They kissed their mother and father. Then they kissed me. I was aware of two successive gusts of a sweet and dreadful perfume; and off they went.

I rode home to Elmbury. My horse was tired, and it was a bitter cold night, with sleet in the north wind; but I was warmed by laughter and cheered by a comfortable sense of the fitness of things. When I had stabled my horse I went to the Swan, and found the Colonel sitting in his usual chair. He'd just been duck-shooting and was very wet. Steam rose from his shoulders as he dried himself before the fire: a little miasma of his own creating. There was a pleasant smell of Harris tweed. He swallowed a large whisky and as he grinned contentedly his scarlet face fell into multitudinous creases: 'Wet, me boy, wet. Whisky inside and water out.'

Then he looked at me curiously. He began to laugh. Miss Benedict, the middle-aged, tight-lipped, prim little barmaid, looked at me too, but without laughter. 'What have you been up to?' said the Colonel.

'Hunting. We had a good run from Brensham Hill. We killed—'

'Hunting!' roared the Colonel, and his glorious laughter shook him as gusts of wind an old tree. 'Hunting! Well, I've heard it called a lot of things—'

Then I saw my face in the glass over the mantelpiece. On my right cheek in post-office red was the print of Meg's kiss; and on my left, in a completely different colour, a sort of orange-tawny which was fashionable at the time, was the impression of Mimi's.

When the pantomime ended the girls returned to Brensham. The experience hadn't 'turned their heads' as Mr

Trentfield had feared it would; but it had given them what their mother darkly described as Ambition, and Mimi was determined to go into Musical Comedy, while Meg already saw herself on the films. At village concerts they indefatigably sang and danced, performing what they called a Double Act: the Trentfield Sisters. It was a step, they imagined, towards stardom. Meanwhile they continued to help with the cricket-teas. They dressed themselves up in light flowery frocks and painted their faces so that Dai Roberts Postman, utterly scarified, whispered comments about the whore Jezebel. But there wasn't a scrap of harm in either of them; and you can imagine what a devastating effect they had upon the younger members of the visiting teams, and upon our own hobbledehoys, who when they sat down to tea found themselves suddenly confronted with the pantomime smile of Mimi and the Hollywood make-up of Meg, and enfiladed by the sidelong glances of Sally Doan.

The Spectators

There has always, I suppose, been a goggle-eyed spectatorial multitude who have watched with enjoyment, in the fashion of the age they lived in, the throwing of Christians to lions, the baiting of bears and bulls, the burning of martyrs, the hanging of malefactors, and the bloody pummelling between heavy-weights with naked fists. There has also, I am sure, since the first primitive hunter grew stiff in his joints, been a company of old men, past-masters of their various sports and games, who have delighted to watch the young upstarts throwing the javelin, shooting the arrow, wrestling, boxing, footballing, cricketing, and to recollect how much better they did these things in *their* young days. But the emergence of a huge class of able-bodied people who actually prefer to watch other people playing the games which they could, if they liked, play themselves is a recent phenomenon. The young men who 'follow' football-teams surely represent something new and something contemptible. Luckily it is a phenomenon of the cities rather than of the countryside. At Brensham the people who didn't play cricket had something better to do than to watch it. They fished in the river, caulked their boats, poached rabbits, weeded their gardens, mowed their lawns, rode their bicycles or motor-bicycles, took their wives to the pictures or their girls into the mowing-grass. Therefore our matches never attracted any considerable number of spectators. I can only remember three fairly regular ones: Goaty Pegleg, the Colonel, and the Mad Lord.

Goaty Pegleg, you will remember, lived in the first cottage on the way up the hill, at the end of the steep stony lane which we always used when we were children. It was two miles from thence to the cricket-field, a bone-shaking road downhill and a back-aching road uphill for a man with a wooden leg. But Goaty Pegleg had been a cricketer in his youth, before he slipped under the wagon wheel at haymaking, and every Saturday and Sunday afternoon in summer he stumped down to watch our games. There was a single bench beneath a shady willow tree beside the pavilion; and here Goaty Pegleg took his ease and watched every ball as keenly as if we had been playing a test match. His attention never flagged; but there was a curious time-lag in his consciousness, he seemed only to become aware of the event some sixty seconds after it had occured. A catch would be taken; and long afterwards, when the batsman, walking out, had nearly reached the pavilion, we would hear Goaty Pegleg's enthusiastic cry: 'He's caught it!' A straight ball would spreadeagle the stumps; and suddenly when the new batsman was taking his guard we would be startled by a

loud clapping, and a throaty cheer from Goaty Pegleg:
'Well bowled, sir!'

The Colonel was a less attentive spectator than Goaty. He
brought a flask with him; and this flask kept him so busy
that he often failed to notice what went on in the cricket-
field. 'Hear you hit a six,' he would say, 'I'm sorry I missed
it; I was having a swig.' He himself was no cricketer; his
unflagging pursuit of animals, birds and fishes had left him
no time for chasing balls. Indeed he only came to watch our
matches during those brief intermediate seasons when there
was nothing to kill, and stayed only for so long as the pubs
were closed; but I think he enjoyed himself, for he liked
Mrs Hartley's hams and meat-pies and he delighted to flirt in
a very courteous and old-fashioned way with Mimi, Meg and
Sally Doan. They loved him, of course; everybody loved
him. I often wondered why, though I loved him as much as
anybody. At first sight he was just a peppery old man who
drank too much whisky; a rather ugly old man, with a
purple pimply nose and a tobacco-stained walrus moustache.
But of course he was much more than that: a kind of greatness clothed him, though I was never able to define it nor
to decide wherein his greatness lay. He had, beneath his
peppery manner, a beautiful courtesy; but so did many
other old gentlemen of his generation. He had a huge sense
of fun, and a twinkle in his blue eyes, and his laughter
bubbled like a spring, was such laughter as the Greeks called
Ionian because it reminded them of the mirth and music of
the mountain streams. But other men, after all, possessed
merry blue eyes and laughed gaily. I think perhaps the
Colonel's greatness had something to do with the fact that
he belonged more completely than anybody else to the fields,
woods, rivers which were his home. He knew the ways of
each thing that ran, swam, crawled or flew not as a man
who has learned them but as if by instinct. And by instinct

too he knew the country people, the carter with bent back leading the horses home after ploughing, the women working in the mangold-fields, the country craftsman laying a hedge, he knew them and was one with them as he knew and was one with the animals. He didn't need to patronize them nor sentimentalize them; he knew what went on in their minds and he had the enormous all-embracing compassion which comes only from complete understanding.

Compassion: perhaps that was the secret of his greatness. His compassion extended to all living things even – though this may sound absurd – to the creatures he hunted. I do not mean that he pitied the fox with the sort of anthropomorphic pity which sentimentalists feel who imagine it suffers the same terror as they would suffer if they were pursued by dogs. He *knew* the fox; he was at once the hunter and the hunted, just as he was farmer and labourer, landlord and peasant because of his compassionate understanding of all. He belonged, as I have said, body and soul to the countryside of Brensham; as if its streams and rivers had run in his veins, its meadows had clothed him, he had grown old with its trees.

At our cricket-teas he was, perhaps, outside his environment and the contrast between our white flannels and his old green tweeds was so striking that strangers would ask: 'Who is that old man of the woodland?' seeing in him at once, as I in my boyhood had seen, a sort of elderly Robin Hood. He wore a hat which was the wonder and the admiration of everybody who gazed upon it, except Mrs Hartley, who was a tidy-minded person, waging ceaseless war against dust and cobwebs with a duster in one hand and a broom in the other: Mrs Hartley was heard to say that she'd like to burn it because it bred germs. It was a deer-stalker hat of Victorian pattern, the kind which French cartoonists once supposed English milords to wear. It was at

least fifty years old, and its original colour was no longer
evident but it had weathered unevenly, so that parts of it
were lichenous-grey and parts of it were mossy-green. Here
and there the moth or the mould had got into it, and here
and there the Colonel's sister – he was unmarried – had
ventured to make a tentative darn. But the holes didn't
really matter, for they were covered up – thatched would be
the better word – with a multitude of fishing-flies. The whole
hat bristled with bits of gut, hooks and feathers. There were
mayflies of ancient pattern, march browns, duns, sedges,
olives, coch-y-bonddhus, alders, and there were salmon-
flies as well to add their tinselled brightness, a Jock Scott,
a Thunder and Lightning, a Blue Charm azure as the
kingfisher. When the Colonel sat down to tea, keeping his
hat on because of the sun, we would delightedly watch the
effect upon the members of the visiting team, who could
scarcely take their eyes off the preposterous thing, except
when Mimi's stagey smile or Sally's brown eyes momentarily
exercised a more powerful attraction.

These visitors must have carried away the impression that
Brensham folk were curiously eccentric in the matter of
clothes; for our third spectator, the Mad Lord, generally
had the appearance of a scarecrow. Indeed, they always
had difficulty in believing that he was a lord: an incredulity
which they shared with the numerous creditors, duns, and
bum-baillies who now perpetually plagued him. Poor
wretches, they could never rid themselves of an uncomfortable suspicion that the tatterdemalion figure was not the
lord, but the lord's cowman. Nor did his manner do much to
reassure them, for he always welcomed them kindly and
they were unused to friendly welcomes. 'My dear fellow,'
he would say, 'I perfectly understand that you will have to
stay at my house during the period of the distraint, but the
trouble is there's simply nothing to eat except rabbits –

which grow rather freely upon the place as you can see – and I shall be positively ashamed of the wretched hospitality which is all I can offer you.' In any case there was precious little to distrain upon; for his furniture, it was said, remained only by the grace of a moneylender from London. The house and lands had been mortgaged long ago. After a brief look-round the duns like disappointed vultures took themselves off; and the bum-baillies soon grew tired of rabbit and reported to their masters that the proceedings were a waste of money. Somehow or other – we never quite knew how – Lord Orris kept out of the County Court and the Bankruptcy Court and, possessing practically nothing nor desiring anything more than he had, continued to live happily amid his ruin and his rabbits, ambitious to receive a few pounds from his quarterly rentals only that he might immediately give them away to the first beggar who came along.

About the time I am writing of he had just scandalized the village by making over three good pastures to a good-for-nothing fellow who was one of his tenants. In justification of this foolish action he had pleaded that the gift had cost him nothing; since the man had never in seven years paid him a penny of rent. He had also, during a hard winter, granted the right of collecting firewood to the Fitchers and Gormleys, who often camped in their caravans uninvited upon his estate; and those gipsyish families, taking him too literally, had not only cut down most of the coppice which adjoined his garden but had carried away the garden fence as well.

He lived alone, except for one old and decrepit servant; Jane had gone to school and she generally spent her holidays in the care of an aunt. The duns were his only visitors; for his relations, we understood, were extremely 'sporting' and they measured happiness by the brace or by the pound, according to whether they were shooting birds or fishing for salmon. They had long ago ceased to come to Orris Manor, where the sport was beneath contempt, the beds unaired, the plumbing primitive, and where the same dish of boiled or roast rabbit was likely to appear at almost every meal.

Perhaps, therefore, the old man grew lonely; at any rate he delighted to visit our cricket-matches, at which he would appear on horseback wearing on hot days a panama and on cooler ones a curious cycling-cap with a button on the top of it, which must have been contemporary with the Colonel's deerstalker. Beneath an ancient black coat, going green with age, he wore a yellow hunting-waistcoat and an old-fashioned cravat. His legs were clad in the most deplorable breeches, patched at the seat and in holes at the knees. His boots would have shamed a tramp.

Our visitors would turn their heads to gaze at him, and between overs would ask us:

'Who's that old Guy Fawkes? Is he mad?'

Well, it depended, said Mr Chorlton, upon your standards of judgement; and his reply to the visitors' question, as he walked between the wickets, must have greatly puzzled them unless they knew their *Hamlet*.

'I think,' Mr Chorlton would say, 'that he's only mad nor'-nor'-west.'

The Match against Woody Bourton

It was delightful to watch these three extraordinary and lovable spectators sitting together on the bench that was only just long enough for them: Goaty Pegleg with his impressive white beard and his wooden peg held out straight in front of him, looking extremely salty and piratical although he'd never seen the sea, nor, in fact, travelled more than twenty miles from Brensham; the Colonel in his green tweeds which merged into the leafy background so that his figure lacked definition and you only noticed the fire-red, gnome-like face, the badger-grizzled moustache, the bright humorous blue eyes; and the scarecrow lord whose panama hat had not worn as well as the Colonel's deerstalker, so that he gave the impression of having, literally, straws in his hair.

I remember a match at which I too was a spectator, and sat on the grass at the feet of these three, because I had sprained my ankle in a fall from my motor-bike. I remember it better than all the other matches, perhaps because the looker-on sees most of the game, or perhaps because it had such a comic and glorious ending, or perhaps again because it happened on the loveliest June day you could possibly imagine, a day of blue and green and gold, and of light breezes, gillyflower-scented, and lullaby sounds of bees, wood-pigeons and faraway cuckoos. The sky was immaculate, hedge-sparrow-egg-blue; the mowing-grass rippled in all the water-meadows along the river and like green foam were the leafy orchards on the lower slopes of the hill. Buttercups along the unmown edges of our ground were a frieze of gold which gilded white cricket-boots and the turn-ups of flannel trousers.

The match was against a team called Woody Bourton and it was a match we particularly wanted to win; for the plain reason that we detested Woody Bourton, whose captain was a dull humourless stone-waller, whose one-eyed umpire had never been known to give an lbw against his own side, and whose wicket-keeper appealed almost ceaselessly in a cracked voice like that of a raven prophesying doom. Do not let yourself be misled by romantic writers into the belief that village cricket is played in a cheerful, 'sporting' spirit of 'Never mind who wins'. I have said that when we took the field we were Brensham going to war. Therefore we minded very much who won. And especially we should mind if we were defeated by Woody Bourton who were known to us as Bloody Bourton. They had beaten us (or, as some said, their umpire had beaten us) the previous year; and we thirsted for revenge.

But from the first ball, which took Mr Chorlton's off stump out of the ground, things went ill with us. Sir Gerald Hope-Kingley, who was next in, ran out Mr Mountjoy, who shortly afterwards ran out himself. ('Like two old hens scampering up and down the wicket they are,' commented Dai.) Sammy Hunt batted for a while with the heroic determination of one who maintains a crumbling citadel against an innumerable enemy; then the wicket-keeper appealed for a catch and up went the loathéd umpire's cigarette-stained finger. Sammy walked slowly back, his bald head bright scarlet, which meant, we rightly guessed, that he was furious about the verdict. Alfie went out, had his stumps knocked flying, and returned to spread alarm and despondency among 'the boys'. 'He's bowling helluva fast,' said Alfie, who frequently employed this curious adjective. Banks, who batted next, was so cast down by Alfie's report that he jumped out of the way of his first ball, which took the bails off.

So far we had lost five wickets for thirty runs, most of which were byes off the fast bowler. Then there was a brief gallant stand by Briggs and Billy Butcher. Briggs for once in a way forgot his ambition to chop every ball County-fashion between the slips; he threw caution to the winds, took hold of his bat by the top of the handle as one would hold a sledge-hammer – and used it as a sledge-hammer. He had a private reason for disliking the Bloody Bourton captain: the man was Conservative Agent for the constituency. So when Briggs smote the ball, he felt that he was smiting the

Tories. Thus inspired he walloped it three times to the boundary and once over the willow trees: three fours and a six, twenty-four runs for Brensham, four hearty blows struck for the proletariat.

Billy, as it happened, was suffering from an appalling hang-over: he'd had a bad bout which had lasted three days and hadn't yet, we suspected, come to an end. But he cocked his cap at a defiant angle and jauntily took his guard, brandished his bat at the first ball in a devil-may-care gesture, missed it altogether, and received the ball on the inside of his thigh. It came quick off the pitch, and it must have hurt badly; but Billy only grinned, pointed his bat at the fast bowler, and called out: 'Hey, mind my courting tackle, if you please!' This made the bowler laugh, and brought a faint smile even to the sombre face of the Bloody Bourton captain. The next ball was a loose one, and Billy cut it over slip's head for an accidental four. Encouraged, he began to play the fool, and his clowning provoked, irritated and thoroughly put off the opposing players, who dropped him twice and let him make several runs from overthrows. Then, unexpectedly in the middle of his clowning, the poetry appeared. Billy would have been a very fine batsman indeed if he could only have achieved the necessary coordination between hand and eye; the whisky got in the way of that. Today, however, he suddenly pulled himself together and made three successive strokes in which the timing was quite perfect. They were sublime: they were a poet's strokes. The first was a drive through the covers which flowed like a slow river with lovely, lazy grace. The next was a cheeky glance to leg carried out as casually as if it had been an impertinent aside during a serious conversation. The third was a glorious pull off his middle stump made with a sort of despairing gaiety, a laughing challenge to the gods, a wild unorthodox defiant shot which you realized,

if you knew him well, was Billy cocking a snook at the world.
The ball went sailing over the brook and into the buttercups
beyond. 'Oh, lovely, lovely, lovely!' cried Lord Orris,
clapping his thin pale hands. The Colonel, wiping the
mouth of his flask, muttered: 'By God, I'll have a drink on
that one,' and did so. A full half-minute later Goaty Pegleg,
travelling slowly in the Fourth Dimension, declared loudly:
'He's hit a six.'

But the effort of coordination had been too much for
Billy. He failed to see the next ball until it hit his pads,
which were plainly in front of the wicket. 'Howzat?'
croaked the Raven, and Joe after a moment's hesitation to
show Bloody Bourton that he could have got even with
their umpire if he had liked, reluctantly gave Billy out.
After that the innings soon ended; three hobbledehoys,
unlucky victims of Alfie's press-gang, made three runs
between them and Briggs, trying to hit another six for
Labour, was caught in the deep. Brensham was all out for
seventy-nine and the teams came in to tea.

I remember the cuckoo which called all teatime from a
willow tree in Cuckoo Pen; and the background of bees and
wood-pigeons and gillyflower scent on the soft light air. I
remember the Colonel's Ionian laughter at some remark of
Billy Butcher's, and old Orris' gentle manners and gentle
smile. I remember Mrs Hartley's ham with the golden
breadcrumbs on it, and a ridiculous garden-party hat which
Mimi wore, and Meg confiding her film ambitions to Mr
Chorlton who listened gravely and didn't smile even when
she said: 'They told me I was ever so photogenic.' I remember Sally Doan plying Billy with meat-pies and whis-
pering to him urgently: 'Now you must *eat*' – and I
remember wondering if she were in love with him. How
absurd and disastrous if she were! But then Joe Trentfield,
who'd been a Sergeant-Major before he took the Horse

Narrow, looked at his watch and said: 'Come along, boys! Late on parade!' and Sammy led our team out into the field.

Now Bloody Bourton had an hour and a half in which to score eighty runs. They could have done it easily; but being Bloody Bourton they scratched and scraped and niggled and fiddled about, as Dai put it, so that half past five – we drew stumps at six, which was opening-time – they had only scored forty for the loss of four wickets. The game looked like ending in a dreary draw; but Bloody Bourton, realizing too late that they would have to score much faster in order to have a chance of winning, suddenly began to hit; and hitting was not in their nature. After Mr Mountjoy had missed an easy catch, because he was listening to the curlews and the drumming snipe in the meadows beyond Cuckoo Pen, Alfie Perks took two wickets in the same over. And still the Bloody Bourton batsmen went out for the runs. A curious sort of desperation had overtaken them; for they delighted as a rule to make pernickety shots along the ground, to score in singles, and to keep their opponents running about in the hot sun for two or three hours while they enjoyed themselves in their prim puritanical way. But now they waved their bats wildly at every ball and called each other frantically for short runs. I heard Mr Chorlton say to Mr Mountjoy between overs: *Quem Deus vult perditur, prius dementat*; and sure enough next ball he was able to stump a batsman who had run halfway down the pitch to one of Alfie's leg-breaks and missed it altogether.

Six wickets for fifty-one, and twenty minutes to go! Sammy, who must be in the forefront of the battle always, put himself on to bowl, pounded down to the wicket with his bald head flaming, and yorked his man with the last ball of the over. Then Billy missed a catch; and our hearts sank. 'It iss the whisky and the pubs and the profane goings-on,' said Dai primly, 'that iss the ruination of cricket in Brensham!' We suffered another set-back a moment later, when Mr Chorlton appealed for a catch and the one-eyed umpire (who might have been blind in both eyes, and stone-deaf as well, for all the notice he took of our appeals) remained motionless as if rooted to the ground, stared stonily in front of him, and took no notice. The Bloody Bourton captain, taking heart, scored a couple of fours, and sixty went up on the score-board. Things looked bad; but a few minutes later Sammy took another wicket for a yorker and at twenty past six the ninth man was stumped by Mr Chorlton. The last man walked out to the wicket as slowly as he dared and as eagerly as if he went blindfold towards the scaffold, snicked a two and a four off Sammy, and got a present of another four from one of Sir Gerald's overthrows. The score was seventy-two when Alfie bowled a long hop to the Bloody Bourton captain, who astonished even himself by hitting it for six.

This was the last over, and Bloody Bourton wanted two runs to win. Even the Colonel sat up tensely and put his flask away in his pocket. Everybody was on his toes with the solitary exception of Briggs, who was standing deep at long-on where for a long time he had had nothing to do. I noticed a faint blue haze hanging about him in the still evening air; I looked again, and perceived that Briggs was lighting his pipe.

Alfie came up to the wicket with his familiar hop, skip and jump, tousled fair hair falling into his eyes. The Bloody Bourton captain, whose success in hitting a six had gone to his head, ran down the pitch and hit the ball a full toss. He caught it awkwardly high up on the splice of the bat but it was a hefty clout all the same, and the ball flew towards long-on. Everybody looked at Briggs; but Briggs, with his big hands cupping a match, was still puffing at his pipe.

The whole team yelled at him. Sammy shouted terrible sea-oaths at the top of his voice. I shouted, the Colonel shouted, even Lord Orris shouted in his small piping voice. Only Goaty Pegleg, who had not yet tumbled to what was happening, remained silent. At last Briggs looked up, and saw the ball falling towards him. He did not move. Without hurry he put the box of matches into his left pocket and the pipe into his right pocket. Then, as one who receives manna from heaven he extended his enormous hands in front of him. The ball fell into them, the strong fingers closed as if they would squeeze it out of shape. Finally, still without hurry, he removed his pipe from his pocket lest it burn his trousers.

When the cheering was over there was a little silence while Joe Trentfield pulled up the stumps and the team came back towards the pavilion. Then Goaty Pegleg announced in a loud voice *urbi et orbi*: 'He's caught it! We've won!' as if he were an astronomer who watches the stars through a telescope and sees, a hundred light years after the event, the flaming destruction of a far-distant sun which, at the moment of earth-time when he witnesses it, has long been black and dead.

So off go Bloody Bourton with perfunctory handshakes and insincere smiles and with black hatred in their hearts. 'It was a good game,' we say, rubbing it in. 'Just the right sort of finish,' they agree without enthusiasm. Mr Mountjoy hurries off to his Evening Service – he's two minutes late already. The Colonel mounts his motor-bike and chugs off towards the Swan. Lord Orris untethers from the gate Tom Pearce's grey mare and rides slowly back towards his ruined mansion. Goaty Pegleg stumps away, the girls wash up the tea-things, Mrs Hartley puts back her ham in its muslin bag. The persistent cuckoo, whose voice is breaking already, calls his last throaty cuck-cuck-cuck-oo from the top of the willow tree.

'And now,' says Sammy Hunt, wiping the sweat-beads off his bald head, 'now for a pint at the Adam and Eve, and a game of darts!'

PART THREE

THE DARTS PLAYERS

Three Pubs – The Adam and Eve – The Language of Darts – The Railway – The Compleat Engine-driver – Trains and Charabancs – The Trumpet – The Horse Narrow – The Landlord – A Social Revolution – Lord Orris' Daughter – We Do See Life – The Purge for Poetry – The Flood – We Band of Brothers

Three Pubs

SOME BIGOTED mean-spirited calculating ass who had probably never stepped inside a pub in his life once wrote a letter about Brensham's pubs to the *Elmbury Intelligencer and Weekly Record*. He signed himself 'Statistician' and his theme was that a single Licensed House should be sufficient for the drinking needs of what he was pleased to call 'approximately one hundred adults of the male sex'. The other two pubs, he suggested, were 'redundant'.

He seemed to suppose that the more pubs there were, the more we should drink, as if a man should say that the more petrol pumps there are by the roadside the more often will a motorist fill up his tank. It was sheer nonsense, of course; but we were very angry indeed at his suggestion that because we had the Adam and Eve, the Horse Narrow and the Trumpet were, in his horrible phrase, 'redundant'.

All three pubs were different and each had a different atmosphere; you might prefer the Adam and Eve to the Horse Narrow or the Trumpet to both, according to your taste, or you might decide on any given evening that the Horse Narrow matched your mood whereas the Adam and Eve didn't. Each had its 'regulars', old faithfuls who would never dream of going elsewhere, but most of us liked a change now and then. You might feel it was an Adam and Eve night, or a Horse Narrow night, or that the company at the Trumpet would be pleasantest; but it was very rarely that you wanted to visit all three. Only Billy Butcher did that, staggering from one to another, and then back to the first, upon his hopeless and terrible pilgrimage.

The Adam and Eve

I suppose I should say, if I tried to differentiate, that the Adam and Eve was the darts players' pub, the Trumpet was the place for a quiet pint and serious conversation, and the Horse Narrow was the rendezvous for those who wanted what we called a bit of jollity: a tune on the piano, a song by Mimi, a pint and a merry tale after closing time with Joe Trentfield. It happened that our cricket-team generally went to the Adam and Eve after matches, because we liked to play darts and because of the wonderful variety of the pickles which Mrs Hartley provided with her bread and cheese.

The landlord, at forty-five, was already a little Falstaff, with a belly which he could only just squeeze through the narrow door in his counter. This was no wonder to us because Mrs Hartley had curious notions about the constitution of men; she was convinced they would faint from starvation unless they devoured at least four enormous

meals a day. She also had her own definition of a snack;
she thought it consisted of a brown cottage loaf, all crusty
and new, with half a pound of fresh butter, yellow as
buttercups, a great hunk of double gloucester cheese,
piccalilli, pickled walnuts, cucumbers, and red cabbage,
with spring onions, lettuce, and radishes if they were in
season. After the cricket-matches, when she thought a
snack would be insufficient, she generally added a meat-pie
or two and a couple of thick slices of ham.

This was all very well for us, who only experienced her
providence once or twice a week. Whether it was good for
her husband was open to doubt; for she continually plied
him between gargantuan meals, not only with her larger
'snacks', but with such occasional titbits as chitterlings,
faggots, cold tongue, or brains on toast, which the poor man
was quite unable to resist. He became, in consequence, a
trifle sluggish. Jim Hartley, you would say, was a very
decent fellow but neither his brain nor his legs worked as
quickly as they used to. This sluggishness was very much
in evidence when it came to a question of turning out the
Voluntary Fire Brigade, of which he was the captain.
Luckily we had very few fires: a hot rick or two, a burning
thatch on bonfire night, a smouldering beam in one of
the old houses, made up as a rule the year's tally. On these
occasions Mr Hartley would look very imposing in his
shining helmet but by the time the old horse had been
coaxed into its bridle and harnessed to the fire engine, and
the engine taken to the fire and the water supply discovered
and the pump set going, the Conflagration, as the *Intelligencer* invariably called it, was 'well under control'.
The neighbours had seen to that. However, there was a
story that once, when the Colonel's old barn took fire,
the *Intelligencer*'s reporter and photographer, driving four
miles from Elmbury, contrived to arrive upon the scene

before Mr Hartley's fire engine which was housed only
four hundred yards away. The barn was blazing merrily
and the Colonel in rage and frustration was dancing about
in front of it like some ancient fire-worshipper. The photographer, whose news-sense was less developed than his
tact, deemed it an inopportune moment to take his picture;
he tactfully walked away up the road in search of the fire
brigade. Shortly it appeared at the trot, with Mr Hartley
in his shining helmet looking like Thor himself. The photographer politely asked if he might take a photograph.
'By all means,' said Mr Hartley, whoa-ing the old mare.
'Pose, men; and when he's ready don't forget to smile.'

Luckily the brigade from Elmbury, which possessed a
motor fire engine, reached Brensham in time to save the
Colonel's barn; and Mr Rendcombe, the Editor of the
Intelligencer, displayed as much tact as his photographer
and forebore to publish the photograph of Jim Hartley's
smile.

Yes, a sluggish man: and yet in one respect he was an
artist, excelling all others. Mr Hartley was the best darts
player I have ever seen; and even at Brensham, where we
prided ourselves upon our darts, he stood out like a Don
Bradman in a village cricket-team, or a great lord among
commoners. He was the only man I have known who
would put three successive darts into the treble-twenty
not as a rare accident, to be celebrated by drinks all round,
but as a commonplace occurrence, not worth celebrating.
He played darts not only with consummate skill and
extraordinary accuracy but with the grace, the assurance,
the artistry of a master. When he squeezed his pot-belly
through the counter-door, and waddled towards the darts
board, he was just a foolish fat oaf of a landlord whose wits
had been dulled by too much roast beef and Yorkshire
puddings; but as soon as he threw the first dart he was

transfigured. He was lordly, he was matchless, he dominated all.

It was not at all surprising, therefore, that the Adam and Eve should be famous throughout the district for its darts. Jim Hartley attracted the darts players to him like a magnet. In his long tap-room we played all our matches, and from there we set off, on winter evenings, to visit pubs elsewhere whose teams had challenged us, the Shakespeare or the Barrel or the Coventry Arms at Elmbury, or the Salutation Inn at Adam's Norton where the darts-match always ended in a sing-song, because the men of Adam's Norton were born to singing as thrushes or nightingales, and the music in their hearts would out, willy-nilly, whenever they had a few pints of beer.

The Language of Darts

If you knew nothing about the game, you would have had a job to understand the talk of the darts players in the spotless bar out of which Mrs Hartley with her duster chased every mote and speck twice a day. For darts has its own esoteric terminology, some of which is common to the whole country and some of which is probably local. It is a language of association, with a bit of rhyming slang mixed up in it. Thus if you score a hundred and eleven – one-one-one – you say 'Nelson': one eye, one arm, and one (let us say) ambition. But if your score is sixty-six it is 'clickety-click', which is simply rhyme. Ninety-nine is 'the doctor': obviously. Twenty-six is 'bed and breakfast' because two and six, in happier days, was the cost of bed and breakfast at a country inn. The left-hand side of the board is known, rather obscurely, as the married side: sixteen and upwards. Thirty-three is 'fevvers' and the reason for that is very obscure indeed; it must have originated in a joke about somebody who couldn't pronounce the sound 'th', for if you ask why thirty-three is associated with 'fevvers' you get the strange reply: 'Firty-free fevvers on a frush's froat.' But why a thrush's throat should be supposed to possess thirty-three feathers, or who took the trouble to count them, I haven't the faintest idea.

A hundred is a 'ton', of course, all over England. Two twos is Jews and two fours is two whores and two tens is two hens and so on. And all over England, surely, if at the end of the game you leave yourself the 'double one' at the top of the board, you are said to be 'Up in Annie's room'. Who was Annie? I wonder; and over what bar did she dwell, and hear the darts thudding on the wall beneath, and what happened up in Annie's room which made the young men and the old men chuckle when their darts flew high?

The Railway

Pubs have characters like people; and there was a factor other than the fame of its darts players which gave individuality to the Adam and Eve and made it different from the other pubs in the village. The main line of the railway ran past it, and Brensham's little station was only a hundred yards away; so the Adam and Eve was not only a village pub but also a railwaymen's pub. The station-master had his morning and evening pint there, pulling out his great turnip-watch every time a train went by; our only porter spent a good deal of time there, as he could afford to do, since the even tenor of his life was interrupted by only four stopping trains a day; and at noon the gangers came in and ordered pints of cider, sat down in the corner and had their bait.

Since Brensham lay in a backwater, well away from the main road which passed through Elmbury, the railway was its principal means of contact with the urban world. When the villagers travelled far afield they went by train; and our summer visitors, mostly anglers from Birmingham who held their fishing contests in our river, generally arrived by train instead of by charabanc. Now whereas the impact of charabancs upon a village is a defiling thing, for they are devouring monsters which destroy the rural atmosphere without putting anything in its place, the impact of the railway has a very different result. The railway is not sterile like the charabancs; it does not, like them, destroy and then vanish, mosstrooper-fashion, but it remains to become part of the village, bringing indeed new life to the village, in the shape of the community which serves it. Thus Brensham wasn't urbanized by the railway; instead the railway at Brensham was made rural. The station master married a Brensham girl and cultivated a typical Brensham garden, all hollyhocks, peonies, and rambler roses, with gillyflowers on the wall. The porter had been born in Brensham, and so had many of the platelayers and gangers; others, who walked each day down the line, tapping the rails, inspecting the sleepers, trimming the hedges along the top of the cutting, were men from neighbouring villages who spoke our speech and thought our thoughts and often played darts with us in the Adam and Eve. Thus the railway had become an integral part of the pattern of Brensham life, with the orchards, the market-gardens, the river, the cricket-field, and the pubs.

The section of permanent way which ran north and south from Brensham was said to be one of the longest straight stretches in the country. The expresses gloriously thundered along it at seventy-six miles an hour, and more than a score of times in each twenty-four hours the glasses rattled in Jim Hartley's bar, and the old pub shook with the tremor of their passing. The gangers who looked after this very fast and important sector were justly proud of the permanent way or, as they called it, the road. They would lean on their picks and watch the express go by, hammer hammer along the lines they'd laid, seventy-six point five miles an hour for five and three-quarter miles with never a curve or a gradient, they would listen for the slight change in the rhythm as the train passed over the bridge, the huge and splendid *snort*! as it roared through the station; and they would think 'She couldn't do that if it weren't for us. She couldn't touch seventy-six if the road wasn't perfect.' I knew two of these men fairly well: George Hard-castle and David Groves. Both were oldish men; both had worked on the Brensham road since their boyhood. At fifty-five they walked, on the average, ten miles a day down the line; and the length of their stride even when they were walking along the village street was the exact unvarying distance between the sleepers so that you could tell they were gangers by the curious rhythm of their pace. Both were men of enormous integrity; their job was a labouring job but they did it with a craftsman's pride. The line which to the rest of us was no more than two sets of rails running through a cutting and along an embank-ment was to them as diverse as a landscape; they knew it yard by yard and from yard to yard it was variable, here was a sandy patch, here was a bit of gravel, here was clay, here was a wet stretch adjoining a culvert which must be examined every day for the faintest sign of a crack or a subsidence. Nor were they concerned with the road alone; their territory extended to the fence on either side of it, they must scythe the grass in the cuttings, lay the hedges, and make sure that the fences were secure against cattle. It was within their province, even, to trap or ferret the

rabbits which made their buries on railway property. Both
were great rabbiters, and since by custom they were allowed to set their traps and snares in the fields adjoining
the line, they were able to earn a little beer-money in
seasons when rabbits were in demand.

They needed it; for gangers are not very well paid. The
engine-drivers, who were the little lords of the railway
line, to whom Brensham was but a signal and a station and
who thundered splendidly past in their fiery chariots,
earned more than twice as much as David and George;
and who knows whether they carried a heavier responsi-
bility or exercised a greater skill? One day George's sharp
eyes spotted a tiny trickle of fresh soil in the embankment
near to the culvert. There was a very slight crack above it:
only a foot long, scarcely an inch wide, but George suspected trouble and he ran to the signal-box and got on the
telephone. When the four-twenty-eight down express came
along she found the signals against her; she was flagged
over the culvert at five miles an hour. But when George and
his inspector examined the crack afterwards they found it
was both longer and wider, and a new crack had appeared
above it. By day and by night, turn and turn-about,
George and David watched beside that little crack; and
finally the Company sent a special train with two hundred
tons of rubble to shore up the embankment. One winter
morning, when the job was nearly done, David relieved
George at six o'clock. It was dark and cold, and perhaps
George was tired and sleepy from sitting over the brazier.
He set off down the six-foot way to go home. He knew to
the minute, of course, the times of all the passenger trains
which passed along his sector and he certainly knew that
the parcels express was due at six-eleven; but a high wind
was blowing, which roared almost as loud as a train
through the tall elms in the coppice above the embankment.

It happened that there was a light engine coming along the up-line; George saw it in good time and stepped out of its way – into the path of the down express.

David Groves found him later and I don't think he ever quite got over that experience; for a man's body is demonstrated to be a pitifully frail thing when it encounters a great mass of steel hurtling along at seventy-six miles an hour. And George had been his companion and best friend for nearly forty years. He carried on with his job, of course, but we noticed that when he brought his bait into the Adam and Eve he ate alone and in silence; and when the expresses went by with a snort and a rattle he would sometimes start, as if he had suddenly remembered how they could hurl a man out of their terrible way as a man might flick a troublesome fly.

And David began to look old now, at fifty-five. He'd had a hard life, hard from the beginning; for at the age of sixteen he'd been hired to a farmer for a whole year for the sum of eighty shillings. Although he was so patient and uncomplaining, and so slow of speech and unready with a quick answer, you could always rouse him to dispute with you if you spoke of the Good Old Days. 'Maybe they were good for some, sir. I can tell 'ee they weren't for us. Up at five to do the milking, dry bread and a slice of fat bacon for breakfast, then a ten-mile round with the milk, a bite of bread and cheese and a glass of cider, then more milking and another ten-mile round. A bit of a sit-down in the kitchen, a bite of supper, and then a hard bed: seven days a week. I dunno how much butter we helped to make every week, but I know we never tasted it; fat bacon was all the grease we got on our bread.' When he was seventeen he went to work for the railway; and for many years after that his wages as a platelayer were sixteen shillings a week. His wife fell ill, and became in the end a permanent invalid;

his son was a cripple who couldn't earn anything towards his keep. It was always a hard struggle to make ends meet, and David never had a penny to spend on himself. 'They talk about Charity in the Good Old Days,' he would say, 'but I never saw much of it myself. I had sixpence from the parson once or twice, and a bag of coal at Christmas. We didn't often see any meat, and we still never tasted butter!'

But as the years went by wages improved and the working day became shorter, so that he had a chance to dig his garden in the summer evenings; he'd never had time for that before. At the age of fifty-five he was earning a little more than two pounds a week, and would have thought himself comfortably off but for the shadow of old age which lay ahead of him. He'd never been able to save anything; and the company which he had served so long and faithfully provided no pensions for their servants in the lower grades when they were worn out and old. So David couldn't have retired even if he'd wanted to; and he patiently carried on as he'd done ever since he was promoted from platelayer to ganger, 'walking his stretch' every day and in all weathers, on Sundays as well as weekdays, for rather less than fifty shillings. His back became more bent and his legs more stiff from treading the sleepers; but his sharp eyes that could see a rabbit-track in the cutting forty yards away still kept faithful watch along the road for the rot in the timber or the fault in the steel, for the wet patch in the clay or the displaced brick in the culvert or the tell-tale seeping of sand from a crack in the embankment. And thanks to David Groves and others like him the great expresses still roared through Brensham station at seventy-six point five miles an hour.

The Compleat Engine-driver

Those expresses never stopped at Brensham. We set our watches by them, and that was all they meant to us, unless some labouring lad, watching the blurred lights tearing past on a winter's evening, and catching a glimpse of the people in the carriages, who'd been in Scotland perhaps for breakfast and would be in Bristol before midnight – unless some such lad standing in a muddy gateway felt the spirit of adventure stirring within him, and upped and away next morning all because of the swift splendid train.

But for most of the villagers the goods trains were much more important than the expresses; Brensham's prosperity was bound up with them. They carried away in season, to the north and to the south, the strawberries, the cherries, the plums, the apples, the pears, the sprouts, the onions and the cabbages upon which nearly half the inhabitants depended for their livelihood. At plum-picking time there was even a special which picked up a load each day at six-thirty and delivered our Pershores and Victorias to the northern cities in time for market next morning.

Upon one famous occasion Alfie Perks drove this train. It was during the General Strike; and Alfie and several other market-gardeners had volunteered to act as porters and load their own produce into the trucks. Thus it came about that Alfie found himself, on the third morning, temporarily in charge of the station; for the station-master had joined the strikers. The six-thirty duly arrived, but its driver who happened to live at Elmbury, jumped down off his engine and declared that he was sick of being a blackleg and was now going home.

'Hey,' said Alfie, 'you can't do that. What about my lettuces?'

But the driver, bearing the little black box which engine-drivers carry, was already on his way out of the station.

'My mates call me a blackleg,' he declared. 'Can't let my mates down.'

'What about letting down us chaps? My lettuces are helluva perishable,' Alfie shouted after him; but it was no good, he was over the bridge and walking rapidly towards Elmbury. Alfie rang up the Junction, ten miles up the line, and asked them what he should do. They told him that they could find an amateur driver to take the train up north, but they possessed no means of transporting the driver to Brensham. 'If the train could only get to us,' they told him, 'we could probably send it on.'

'How the hell do you expect it to get to you?' asked Alfie, 'call it, and perhaps it will come.' He was angry; he had forty crates of lettuce in his dray and they would be worthless in twenty-four hours. He went back to the engine and talked to the fireman.

'Can you drive this thing?' he asked.

'Yes,' said the fireman. 'It's easy.'

'Well, unless you're going on strike too,' said Alfie, 'you'd better bloody drive it.'

'Can't do that,' said the fireman. 'It's against company's regulations *and* the Union. More than my job's worth.'

'Can you show *me* how to drive it?'

'Sure, I can do that.'

So Alfie loaded up his lettuces and off he went. He'd never even driven a lorry before; in fact, he'd never driven anything but his old horse which looked rather like a rocking-horse and was appropriately named Dobbin. But the fireman condescended to take off the brakes for him, and put them on when the train reached the Junction, and the rest, said Alfie, was helluva easy. There was a shortage of produce in the Manchester markets next day, and his

lettuces made the best price he'd ever had. 'Twas a pity, he
said, the Strike looked like ending; or he'd have bought his
own railway engine and delivered his stuff personally.

Trains and Charabancs

So, you see, the railway brought both tragedy and comedy
to Brensham. Our lives were bound up with it as they were
bound up with the river and the hill. I have seen the effect
of the charabancs and the motors on a main road village
near Elmbury; I have watched them slowly suck its blood
so that in a few years the village had no real life at all
except a kind of spurious weekend life which was that of its
parasites. When they went away on Monday there was
nothing but a sham village, a mere husk, consisting of
petrol-stations, two deserted tea-shops, a pub full of
chromium-plating and ill-kept beer, a tea-garden with
yellow-striped umbrellas over the tables, and Ye Olde
Blacksmythe's Shoppe where an indifferent craftsman made
curios. It was a dead village which on Saturdays and
Sundays and Bank Holidays was grotesquely galvanized
into activity in the fashion of a Zombie. The parasites had
sucked it dry.

But the railway wasn't parasitic on Brensham; instead of
sapping its vitality, it actually made the pulse of the village
beat faster. And it robbed us of nothing, except a few
moments of our quietude now and then. Nor was that a
perceptible theft; for the people who lived along the line
didn't wake up when the midnight express hammered past;
they only woke up if it failed to pass, and listened to the
silence, and looked at their watches, and wondered what
had happened to make it so late.

The Trumpet

The second pub, as you walked down the village from the Adam and Eve, stood close to Mrs Doan's Post Office, and almost opposite the entrance to Magpie Lane. It was bigger than either of the others, and it had a sizable back room where Cricket Club and Farmers' Union meetings and the annual dinners of organizations such as the British Legion were held. It was more modern than the Horse Narrow and the Adam and Eve: it had a garage at the back, and advertised 'Bed and Breakfast, h and c'.

Notwithstanding, it was an unlucky pub. It had had a succession of landlords, some good and some bad, but none of them had managed to make a fair living out of it. This was partly due to its situation in the middle of the village; for the Horse Narrow and the Adam and Eve stood like sentries at either end, and offered a strong challenge to thirsty travellers approaching from either direction. Also, at the time I am writing of, it was suffering from the after-effects of having had for three years the worst landlord in Brensham's history, a villainous, get-rich-quick towny fellow whose notion of a country inn was a place where people from the City spent illicit weekends and were charged double prices for the privilege. In consequence, he spent a good deal of his time giving evidence at the Divorce Court (which he thoroughly enjoyed) instead of attending to his legitimate business in the bar.

Now nobody could say that Brensham was a puritanical village; indeed I think our illegitimate birth-rate was rather high and we certainly saw little harm in our young lovers' midsummer mischief so long as they did not do too much damage to the crops. We disapproved of the dreary divorcees at the Trumpet not because of their morals, which were no concern of Brensham, but because of their manners, which grossly offended us. So the Trumpet's few 'regulars' began to drift away to the other pubs, and although the landlord didn't mind this in the summer he began to notice the effect of it in the long, dark winter evenings, when there were no weekenders and even if there had been the gloomy spectacle of Brensham's flooded river, muddy lanes and fields of rotting sprout-stems would have promptly ended their romance.

The landlord now began to grow jealous of the other two pubs, whose bars were full of darts players even on the wettest and coldest nights. So one evening when he had closed his bar promptly at ten – there were no customers to turn out of it – he took a walk down to the Horse Narrow and was gratified to find that the lights were still on in the bar. He peered through the window and saw Joe serving drinks, Mimi playing the piano, and a dozen villagers enjoying a sing-song. The clock over the bar stood at ten-twenty. Joe, who enjoyed the singing, had forgotten the time; and he was never very particular about prompt closing anyway.

The landlord of the Trumpet hastened back to his pub and rang up the police-station. His towny voice was sly and ingratiating. He believed in keeping in with the police.

'Mr Banks,' he said, 'I'm going to give you a tip.'

'Oh, yes?' said Banks, surprised and on his guard. 'What is it?'

'Just take a walk down the street and you'll see.'

It was a beastly night, cold and drizzly, and Banks had been sitting in his slippers before a good fire. He said rather sharply:

'I can't act on that. Tell me what's the matter and I'll go and deal with it,'

'Well, it's like this, Officer,' said the wretched landlord.

'I happened to be passing the Horse and Harrow a few minutes ago – ten-twenty to be exact – and I'm sorry to say that there's Goings On there. I don't like to let a fellow landlord down but what's fair for one is fair for all. There were drinks being served, and music.'

Banks remained silent. As he told some of us afterwards, he was doing a bit of quick thinking. After all, Joe Trentfield was his father-in-law.

'Music *and* singing,' whined the landlord into the silent telephone. And then, losing his head a bit, perhaps, because he still got no answer, he made a most foolish and disastrous statement:

'I thought,' he said, *'that you might like the chance of making a good cop.'*

A good cop! 'Leaving out altogether,' said Banks, when he told us about it, 'the fact that I'd have copped my own father-in-law, did the fool really believe that I'd think it a good cop to get *any* landlord in the village into trouble – or anybody else for that matter?' Banks had been village policeman for eight years; Brensham had tamed him. So he said coldly:

'Thank you for your information, but as it happens I know all about it. Mr Trentfield warned me that he was having a party tonight. It is perfectly in order.'

'But he hasn't got an extension!' wailed the miserable wretch.

'No,' said Banks firmly. 'It's a private party. Nobody is paying for drinks.' He rang off. Next day he went to see Joe and put the fear of God into him; he also visited the Adam and Eve and warned Jim Hartley to be careful. He wasn't very discreet; I think he felt that for once in a way discretion didn't accord with justice. So he said frankly: 'I'm warning you only because we've got a tell-tale among us.' That was enough. Joe knew who it was, and Jim

Hartley guessed. Everybody in the village knew by closing-time that night.

Now Brensham was a remarkable village in this fashion: although it possessed, I think, as diverse a collection of inhabitants as you'd find anywhere in England, it was nevertheless more of an entity than any other community I have known. Its strange assortment of individualists had a way of getting together about any major issue and acting as one man. 'They hangs together,' Pistol had said to me; and he was right. Brensham hung together now. The question wasn't debated in public; there was no common discussion or common agreement about it; but every individual in Brensham made his individual decision to boycott the Trumpet for as long as the treacherous landlord remained there. Even Billy Butcher, in his most drunken moments, staggered past it with his head in the air. The landlord never again sold so much as a half-pint to any of our villagers. He couldn't live on weekenders and we broke him in six months. When he left he had a sale, but no one belonging to Brensham attended it. The only bidders were two or three dealers from Elmbury who formed a ring between them and bought up his few sticks of furniture for a song.

The Trumpet's next landlord was as decent a fellow as you could find; but the pub remained an unlucky one. Its 'regulars' had left it, and become 'regulars' at the other pubs; being creatures of habit they were unwilling to make another change. It was more difficult to get the trade back than it had been to lose it; and when the new landlord's wife died, and he could no longer provide bed-and-breakfast for the occasional motorists, he was hard put to it to make a living.

We sometimes called at his pub after cricket-matches, out of friendship and because we were sorry for him; but although he looked after his beer well and kept his bar clean we were never entirely at ease there. It had neither the homeliness of the Adam and Eve nor the boisterous gaiety of the Horse Narrow. It was just a place for drinking in; and although that may be the teetotallers' idea of a pub, it was very far from being ours.

The Horse Narrow

Nor was it Joe Trentfield's. It had been his ambition all his life to be an inn-keeper; and the reason, as he truthfully said, was because he liked to see people enjoying themselves. He had saved up during nearly twenty years of soldiering in order that he might gratify this simple ambition when he retired. Now he had his reward; for none but a churl or a misanthrope could fail to enjoy himself at the Horse Narrow. The atmosphere in the bar was rather like that of a large family party; and what was particularly enchanting about it was that the family obviously enjoyed it as much as the guests. Joe's round red face positively shone with happiness; Mrs Trentfield's bosom heaved with laughter like a balloon spinnaker filled with wind; Mimi giggled and sang, Meg giggled and strummed. No Happy Family could have been happier.

'I likes to see people having fun,' said Joe. 'I likes to see a bit of life,' said Mrs Trentfield. They weren't very finicky about what constituted Fun and Life, so long as it warmed the cockles of their hearts. Mrs Trentfield enjoyed a bawdy joke or a naughty song as much as anybody; and, when she listened to either, the balloon spinnaker filled and shook and swelled and billowed as if it would burst. As for Joe, he was in the habit of declaring: 'The Horse Narrow is Liberty 'All.' Even when Billy Butcher, being in the destructive stage, took him at his word and started pitching glasses at the darts board, Joe merely laughed, and Mrs Trentfield's only comment as she swept up the pieces was: 'Well, we do see Life.'

The very structure of the Horse Narrow matched its landlord's free-and-easy character. There was a great apple tree outside it, which dripped pink petals on the doorstep in spring and tapped with its twigs upon the top-storey windows whenever there was a wind. The half-timbered, deep-thatched building had been added to from time to time by various local builders, so that it had a crooked, lopsided and rather comical appearance. The eaves jutting out over the small bedroom windows looked like beetling eyebrows; and Joe had beetling eyebrows too. The crazy inn sign, with its horse and arrow, completed the impression which the place gave of belonging to phantasy.

The same sort of delightful disorder was apparent within. There were numerous low beams in awkward places, upon which strangers were apt to bang their heads. When they did so, Joe roared with laughter. His catholic notion of what constituted Fun included all minor misfortunes of that kind. Generations of happy-go-lucky builders had contrived the various additions and alterations in a spirit of rough humour which beautifully matched Joe's. Some of the doors were too narrow, and opened the wrong way; when Mrs Trentfield's bosom became jammed in them, Joe nearly split his sides. The only bathroom was placed on the opposite side of the house from the bedrooms; in order to get to it visitors and members of the family had to pass through the bar. The sight of Mimi scampering through in her dressing-gown, or Meg running the gauntlet of the young men with her hair in curlers, was an unfailing source of merriment for Joe. Another was associated with a freak of the plumbing. Every time the lavatory plug was pulled, it emptied a tank immediately over the bar, which refilled itself with a curious gurgling noise. Joe called it Minnie haha, Laughing Water; and it never failed to set him going so that the chuckle in the ceiling seemed like an echo of his great gusty laughter, it was as if the very building shared his mirth.

The walls of the bar were decorated with the strangest assortment of pictures and curios. There were coloured photographs of Mimi and Meg in their exiguous panto-mime dresses, looking very pink and shiny and as unreal as an adolescent's dream; yet if you glanced at Mimi and Meg you realized at once that the photographs were likenesses, the sisters were indeed an embodiment of the image in the mind of the awakening boy: a sort of synthesis of girls.

There was also a photograph of Joe as a Regimental Sergeant-Major, and one of Mrs Trentfield on her wedding-day which suggested that Mimi's taste in hats might be hereditary. There was a pair of antlers, one of Joe's trophies from Africa, which he had seen fit to decorate with an old top-hat. There was an improbable-looking stuffed pike in a glass case and a live parrot in a cage, and there were a number of innocently-vulgar postcards, chiefly showing fat women in bathing dresses, which the unerring instinct of Joe's best friends had prompted them to send him from Weston-super-Mare. Upon the shelf behind the bar were some more of these postcards, the ones which Joe deemed unfitted for display upon the walls, and a piece of wood-carving representing the Long Man of Elmbury who was in some ways an even more impressive figure than the better-known Long Man of Cerne Abbas. On this shelf also there was generally a collection of malformed potatoes, parsnips, tomatoes, and vegetable marrows which local gardeners had brought to the Horse Narrow in the certainty that they would make Joe laugh. A potato shaped like a manikin, a parsnip resembling a mermaid, a Pompeian broad bean or cucumber – these curiosities would afford him endless delight and he would hold them up to show his customers, or demonstrate their peculiar qualities to his wife, with such a happy grin on his red face that even a prig or a Puritan would be bound to join in the laughter. Up from his very boots would come Joe's deep chuckle and Mrs Trentfield heaving in front like a pouter pigeon would laugh till she cried, and the Echo in the ceiling perhaps would answer them, so that their laughter before it died away was reinforced and renewed. It was the laughter, surely, of Chaucer and Rabelais; for it was of the earth earthy, like the comic misshapen vegetable in Joe's hand.

The Landlord

For all his happy-go-lucky manner, Joe took his job as landlord very seriously. He worked far longer hours than most of us; as he said: 'A pub ties you worse nor a dairy herd, for a man can generally find somebody to milk his cows' – whereas it took an expert to milk those casks in the cool dark room behind the bar. Besides, there is more to pub-keeping than that. Joe fulfilled a function in the village much larger than that of mere provider of beer. He was a sort of secular Father Confessor; for if a man wanted to share his troubles or ventilate his grievance or tell a funny story it was ten to one that he'd make his way to the Horse Narrow. There he was certain to find Joe standing behind his well-polished counter, always ready to listen patiently and nod his head understandingly and at the end to put in a wise or comforting word, or if it were appropriate to gladden the storyteller's heart with his thunderous laughter.

And when the talk was general, and the pub became, as

it often did, a sort of village parliament – when the discussion concerned perhaps some question of village politics such as a right-of-way or the water-supply or the drains, Joe found himself in much the same situation as the Speaker: he must keep the peace without taking sides. He never forgot that he was the host and his customers were guests, that all shades of opinion were represented among them, and that it was part of a host's duty not to give offence. I have heard him when the debate became heated sum up both arguments as impartially as a judge.

He had other, more definite duties. For example, he was the village banker; he cashed our cheques, and looked after our savings through the 'club' which held its annual share-out at Christmas. He was also secretary of the local branch of the Sick Benefit Society whose members came to the Horse Narrow every Monday to pay their contributions or draw their sick pay if they were, as the phrase went, 'on the club'. Thus he knew more than the District Nurse about the state of health of everybody in the village; and he was often more prompt than Mr Mountjoy in visiting the sick. If he was too busy to go himself he would send round one of the girls; and if the sick person was badly off they would generally take a present of a pat of butter or half a dozen eggs. Mimi might look like a chorus-girl, and Meg simulate in her dress and make-up the latest film star, but surely no village under the sun possessed two more warm-hearted almoners.

Despite all this, Joe was a 'publican' and therefore in the eyes of the law eternally suspect. He knew well that the merest accident could lose him his licence and his livelihood. He must contrive at all times to diagnose each of the dozen signs of incipient drunkenness, to nip a dangerous argument in the bud, to recognize a child under age (and refuse to serve some chit of a girl who'd larded her face with

make-up until she looked older than her mother!), to persuade his customers to leave peacefully at closing-time. It
would be a black mark against him at the licensing sessions
if the Fitchers and Gormleys had a serious fight in his house;
if 'the boys' too obviously played solo or cribbage for
money; if Mr Sparrow the bookie's runner from Elmbury
was caught outside the pub with a pocketful of betting-
slips; or even if some fool of a lorry-driver who had stopped
for a drink at a dozen other places had his last one at the
Horse Narrow and then ran into a telegraph pole.

In fact, as Joe said with his deep guffaw: 'Judging by the
sort of character and references they want before they'll
let you keep a pub, you has to be an angel; but as soon as
you've got your licence they looks on you as the biggest
bloody rogue alive.'

A Social Revolution

At the time I am writing of, early in the nineteen-thirties, a
remarkable change was occurring in the social habits of the
villagers. Like most English revolutions it happened
gradually and without fuss. It produced the usual grumbles
and the usual rhetorical questions about 'What's the
world coming to?' and a few Diehards expressed the
opinion that it would 'lead to immorality' which in social
revolutions is always the Diehards' last ditch. I refer to a
change in the domestic custom which had started very
much earlier in the cities and towns: the women of Brensham
began to use the pubs.

Of course, it was no new thing for Joe Trentfield or
Jim Hartley to serve women with drinks. There were
always a few old crones who were 'regulars' at one or
other of the pubs; these generally drank stout, or, when

the weather was cold, spiced warm beer which set their tongues wagging fourteen to the dozen. The Fitchers and Gormleys, upon their unwelcome seasonal visits, always brought their womenfolk, who added to the horrors of the subsequent free-for-all by their employment of finger-nails and hairpins. And there was a great gypsyish woman from Adam's Norton called Shooks who descended upon Brensham most Saturday nights and passed from pub to pub like Billy Butcher, a blowsy unpleasing creature resembling a figure out of Hogarth's gin-palace drawings, whose appearance in the Horse Narrow quenched even Joe Trentfield's earthy sense of fun.

But these women were not typical of Brensham; they formed a class of their own. They were disapproved of, laughed at, or accepted with a shrug of the shoulders as part of the Brensham scene; but they certainly did not set a fashion. They were rather a deterrent to other women. 'Go boozing in the Horse Narrow and get like old Shooks? Not I!' The village men would not have dreamed of taking their wives, their girls or their daughters to any of the pubs until about 1930. Then a number of factors began to operate which slowly effected the change.

Mimi and Meg may have had something to do with it. They got up a concert-party of young men and girls, and held their rehearsals at the Horse Narrow in the long room next to the bar. Sometimes these rehearsals went on too long, so that the bar was open before the young people had left. The customers would say 'Give us a song, girls!' and then would buy them a shandy. Gradually it became accepted that Mimi's Girls, as they were called, might be found in the bar at any hour. Their mothers made no great fuss about it; for Mimi and Meg were extremely popular even among those who described them as little hussies, and Mrs Trentfield in spite of her appreciation of a dirty joke

was known to be a motherly person who would see to it
that the girls came to no harm.

Certainly the homeliness and the family-party atmosphere of the Horse Narrow did a lot towards breaking
down the ancient prejudice against taking wives and
sweethearts into bars. Another factor was the example set
by the 'gentry', who had no such prejudice: Mr Chorlton's
niece, who stayed with him in the holidays, always came
along with the team after cricket-matches and played
darts as competently as most of the men; Sir Gerald's
wife and his middle-aged sister often accompanied him to
the Trumpet; and even the parson's two daughters, only
just back from a finishing-school in Switzerland, thought
nothing of taking their numerous young men to the Horse
Narrow and publicly drinking pints of beer.

Then there was the Mad Lord's daughter. She came
down to spend a few weeks with him, one summer holiday,
and on the very first morning she went into the Adam and
Eve, all alone, leaned on the bar, and asked for a Guinness!
We hardly recognized her at first; for since her mother died,
ten years previously, she'd been brought up by her aunt.
We still remembered her as a pale shy child with long hair
rather like Tenniell's pictures of Alice. Now she was up at
Oxford – her aunt was paying, we supposed – and she was a
tall and beautiful girl with nothing of the Alice-look about
her, unless it were in her big and inquisitive grey eyes.

Well, thought the villagers, if the pubs are good enough
for the Honourable Jane, they ought to be good enough for
our wives; if Parson Mountjoy sees no harm in his daughters
drinking pints, maybe we shouldn't object to ours taking a
half-pint of shandy. So the social revolution was gradually
achieved. What was at first a liberty taken by the gentry,
because they stood outside the reach of the usual sanctions,
became in the end a liberty indeed. It was no longer the

function of women to sit at home and wait for the men to come back from the pub – wondering apprehensively whether they'd be drunk or sober, good-tempered or bad. The man's world of pubs and darts and evening talk was immeasurably widened, because women also had their place in it.

Lord Orris' Daughter

Brensham, which had its own sense of values about which it was sure and confident, wasn't an easily shockable village. It wasn't at all shocked, for instance, though it was a trifle surprised, when Jane Orris first walked into the Adam and Eve. However, it was certainly put out when young Jane publicly declared that she was a Communist; and the village took a few weeks to see the matter in its proper perspective.

Probably nobody would have minded if only Jane had been concerned; for she belonged to Brensham, she was one of us even though she had learned unfamiliar ways at Oxford, and since the village believed in individualism and stoutly practised it, she could have declared herself a Seventh Day Adventist if she'd liked and nobody would have minded. From the Mad Lord's daughter we expected no less. What shocked us for a little while – nothing shocked us for long – was not Jane but Jane's young men. They came down every weekend and draped themselves upon the bar at the Adam and Eve or the Horse Narrow. They wore long hair and pink ties and very baggy trousers. They preached to us a doctrine which we found difficult to understand in a manner which insulted us. They were bogus and we knew they were bogus. They patronized, and that, in Brensham, was the unforgivable sin.

For instance, they addressed people like Jeremy Briggs the blacksmith and David Groves the permanent-way ganger by their Christian names. The Colonel could do that, and so could Billy Butcher, and both Jane and I could do it because the village had known us since we were children. But when Jane's foolish young men said 'Have a drink, Jeremy' or 'Tell us, David, are you really content to go on all the rest of your life working for two pounds a week?' it was a breach of good manners and there was an embarrassing silence before Jeremy excused himself and David made some short non-committal reply.

I don't suppose there was much harm in these drawing-room Bolshies, as the Colonel called them. Mr Chorlton, who was tolerant and wise and who knew a great deal about young men, told us that they reminded him of his own undergraduate days. 'We called it Aestheticism then, and now they call it Communism; but it's simply growing pains really. Our Aesthetes, most of 'em, were shooting lions or foxes or fighting in the Boer War a few years later. These Communists will probably be Diehard Tories, God help 'em, before they reach the age of forty. *Plus ça change.*'

'And what about Jane?' I asked him.

He shook his head.

'She's different. There's something authentic there. It isn't part of the fancy-dress which she's put on with an undergraduate's gown. It isn't academic, at all. She's full of righteousness and burning pity and she wants to go on a Crusade. Isn't she splendid? She warms my old heart. Do you know, I was looking at her the other day and I thought: Suppose she'd been born just over a hundred years ago, and born a man, and she went striding down the High with a pistol in one hand and a poem in the other, whom would you see? The young Shelley.'

We Do See Life

We caught a glimpse of that 'burning pity' in the Horse
Narrow one evening soon after Jane came home. It was also
the night of the big autumn flood, when the Colonel was
nearly drowned; and it was the night when Billy Butcher
got more sublimely drunk than I have ever seen him.
Mr Trentfield had frequent occasion to remark 'We do
see Life, don't we?' Townsmen who believe that nothing
ever happens in the country should have been with us on
that first of October.

The evening began quietly enough, with a Cricket Club
meeting for the purpose of 'winding up the accounts for
the past season'. I came in late, on my way home from shooting what was probably Lord Orris' only cock pheasant;
for he had invited me to walk round his land and get
whatever I could of the poacher's leavings. He didn't shoot
himself; he hated killing things. So I took him the cock
pheasant in the hope that it would be a change from his
usual diet of rabbit, though I felt pretty certain that he'd
give it away. I was right. He said: 'How nice of you. And
it's the only one you got, in a whole day's walking through
the rain? Dear, dear; I feel positively ashamed of inviting
you. Those mischievous fellows from Elmbury poach them
all, I'm afraid ; but I can't find it in my heart to blame
them, living in those awful alleys, and unemployed, and
with their wives and children hungry, perhaps . . . And
that reminds me. You won't mind, will you – I know you
won't mind – if we don't actually eat this exquisite thing
ourselves? You see, there's a fellow at the Lodge – he used
to be my cowman as a matter of fact in our palmy days –
whose daughter's just going to have a baby. It's what they
call a mishap, as it happens; she's not married. And that

makes it all the worse for the poor girl, doesn't it? And she's a bit finicky about her food, I'm told; they get like that. So if you *really* wouldn't mind, I'd like to take it along there – as a present from *you*, of course – where it would really be a godsend to the unfortunate child . . .'

Bless his heart, I watched him stump off in the pouring rain down his weedy drive towards the Lodge, admiring the bird's bright plumage as he carried it, and looking as happy as if somebody had left him ten thousand pounds.

It had been raining all day: the second day running of ceaseless driving rain. I was wet through; but it had given me some satisfaction to reflect that the Syndicate, whose guns were pop-popping all day on the other side of the hill, were probably as wet as I was and a good deal colder, since their pheasants were driven to them and they notoriously sped from stand to stand in their big motor-cars. I walked up the hill as far as the larch plantation and had half a mind to poach it; they were saving it, no doubt, for another shoot tomorrow. However, I was Orris' guest and it would have been ill-manners to my host if I had done so. As far as the Syndicate was concerned I had no compunction.

I got to the cricket-meeting at the usual moment of crisis when Sir Gerald, who was Treasurer at the time, was announcing solemnly:

'I am sorry to say that I have to report a deficit on the season of twenty-one pounds five and twopence. This is in addition to the overdraft of thirty pounds which we incurred when we bought the motor-mower—'

Mr Chorlton, who could never resist a quotation, and hardly ever failed to add the source of it, said:

'To owe is a heroic virtue: Rabelais.'

'Our bank manager,' said Gerald drily, 'apparently doesn't agree with Rabelais' corollary: that it is a godlike thing to lend.'

Sammy Hunt, getting down to earth, remarked as he did at this juncture every year:

'We'll have to get up another rummage sale, that's the answer.'

'And a whist drive and dance,' said Jeremy Briggs.

'Aye.' Sammy nodded. 'Alfie will do that, as usual. By the way where *is* our Secretary? I'm sick of keeping the minutes myself.'

Banks said:

'Perhaps he's still looking for Rexy Perks.'

Brensham had a curious custom of referring to dogs by the surnames of their masters. Almost every villager had his dog and generally took great pride in its ability as a retriever, rabbiter, ratter, badger-baiter, house-guard and so on. So they talked of dogs almost as if they were people: 'I hear Bengy Briggs has got distemper,' or 'Rexy Perks has gone all ginger. Alfie must be spraying.'

'He came along to the station this afternoon,' Banks went on, 'to say that Rexy was lost. Very upset, Alfie was.'

Billy Butcher in a loud voice suddenly announced: 'Brothers and sisters, I bid you beware of giving your heart to a dog to tear,' and then giggled. I noticed for the first time that he was very drunk. It had been market day in Elmbury, when the pubs are open all the afternoon.

'Well,' said Sir Gerald briskly, 'I think that's all. I'll write to the bank and put their minds at rest. I'll tell them I'll guarantee the excess, if necessary.'

Soon afterwards the meeting ended and we went into the bar. Alfie arrived, apologetic and disconsolate; he'd bicycled almost all the way to Elmbury, looking in vain for Rexy.

'Nobody ain't seen him,' said Alfie. 'And that's funny, because everybody knows Rexy.' He added: 'It's raining helluva hard. The river's rising fast, and no wonder. It's over the meadows at Dykeham.'

''Twill be a big flood,' said Sammy Hunt, and launched himself immediately into a story about a flood in the Yellow River. Like all his tales, it had no ending. Broad and long as the great Yangtse itself it flowed majestically on, and while we listened bemused to what was surely the story's climax – for no less than a thousand drowning Chinamen were being borne down towards Sammy's ship – there was the briefest hiatus while Sammy remarked that floods reminded him of droughts and droughts of deserts, and lo, before we realized it we were enmeshed in another story which looked like being even longer. Its scene was set in Arabia, Sammy had gone ashore to shoot quail and he was armed only with a twelve-bore when a party of Bedouins attacked him.

'These Bedouins would have liked to hand me over, see, to old Johnnie Turk. It was during the last war, I don't know if I told you? I always liked the Turk funnily enough, always a gentleman. But those Arabs, dirty rats, they'd hand you over to whichever side they thought would pay most, see. And if they took it into their heads to kill you, Lord, I shouldn't like to say what they did to you afterwards! I could never get used to the thought of lying dead like that. 'Twas their women did it. Where was I?'

'Nearly caught by a lot of Bedouins,' said Joe Trentfield helpfully.

'Oh, yes. Well, to cut a long story short, there I was in a little wadi with nothing but my gun, see, when along comes these damned Arabs, twenty of them there must have been but they left some behind to hold their horses. Now on account of the conformation of the ground, as they say, these Arabs had to crawl up the wadi right into my line of fire if they wanted to get me; so I just lay there and waited. And as I waited, I thought, if they kill me, I know what they'll do. Their women will do it. Always have their women handy, the Arabs do. And there I shall be, stretched out on the sand—'

But just as Sammy was about to describe to us the unpleasing appearance of his hypothetical corpse, which as a matter of fact he'd done a good many times before, a car drew up outside and there came in with a blast of cold air and a spatter of rain Lord Orris' daughter. She was hatless and big raindrops ran down her flushed cheeks. Her old mackintosh was torn, and she carried in her arms a bloody bundle. She strode up to the bar and said to Alfie:

'Here he is. I found him in a trap. Those devils with their traps! I'd like to kill them. It's bust his leg, I'm afraid.'

She put Rexy down on the counter. Through the torn flesh of his foreleg I could see a protruding splinter of bone. Alfie stroked him and with a rather painful attempt to sound casual said:

'Yes, it's bust all right. I wonder if we ought to finish him off, Sammy?'

Sammy, who had great gentle hands, picked up Rexy and examined the broken limb.

'I should get a vet,' he said. 'They can do wonderful things with splints nowadays.'

'I'll ring him up,' said Joe, and went out. We heard him in the back-room calling to Mimi to fetch the iodine.

Rexy lay still and whimpered. There was a short silence and then Alfie, who had gone very white, said:

'It was awfully kind of you, Miss Jane.'

'I took him to your house,' she said, 'but they told me you were here.'

'How did you find him?' asked Mr Chorlton.

'I was up on the hill. I love walking in the rain. I got to the larch plantation – you know, your old bug-hunting place, they got it off Father years ago because he owed them some money – and then I remembered that somebody had told me they'd killed off the fallow-deer. I thought I'd go and see. So I went in and then I heard Rexy yelping. I suppose he'd been yelping for hours, and these devils must have heard him because they'd been shooting all day in the coverts just below where he was. But of course they wouldn't care about a dog.'

'Did you have a job to get him out of the trap?' said Banks.

'Well, I did as a matter of fact. He bit me,' said Jane factually. Then we noticed for the first time that she'd a handkerchief tied round her hand.

'Better let me fix it,' said Banks. 'I can do first-aid.'

'It's nothing. We'll put some iodine on it when Joe comes back. But listen: aren't they horrible, unspeakable, beastly?' Jane turned to address us all. She was splendidly and beautifully angry. I knew what Mr Chorlton had meant when he said she wanted a Crusade. 'What can we *do* about them? They're rich and they're powerful and they've got everything they want in the world; and yet they always want more. They've got thousands of pheasants; but they set those cruel traps to catch the vermin in case they should lose half a dozen. And they killed the fallow-deer because they were afraid they might do a few pounds' worth of damage. They were gentle and delicate and graceful; so the Syndicate killed them. They kill everything that's lovely. One day they'll gobble up this village as they're gobbling up my father's land now. They'll squeeze you out one by one, they'll offer you a tempting price for your cottage or your bit of land and if you don't take it they'll break you. Can't we do something, *now*, before it's too late?'

She was so splendid and passionate, I wanted to cheer. Sammy said:

'They'll never get Brensham. We'll see to that.'

'Don't you be so sure,' said Jane. 'My father once said they'd never have the larch plantation.'

'They've got the big guns,' said Alfie. 'They're helluva powerful.'

'Wait till *we* get into power,' said Briggs. 'We'll clip their wings.'

'When you get into power,' said Jane, swiftly, 'they'll clip *your* wings. They've done it twice already.'

'That's all very well, Miss Jane; we never had a clear majority anyhow.' Briggs worshipped Jane but he could never quite forgive her for being Redder than he was. 'Suppose I ask you what you'd do about it if your lot got into power?'

'There wouldn't be any need for us to do anything. If ever we got in we'd go in on a great tide of anger which would sweep the Syndicate and all such things away.'

'Like the French Revolution?' said Mr Chorlton.

'Yes!' said Jane.

'I'm all for it,' said Mr Chorlton with a little smile, 'if you'll cut off the right heads. But people get excited and, well, indiscriminate.'

Jane said:

'Well, I'm going to do *something*, anyhow. While I'm still angry I'm going to drive along to their shooting-box or whatever they call it and tell them what I think of steel traps. I'll go now. Alfie, with all my heart I hope Rexy gets better. Goodbye, everybody.' She turned to Mr Chorlton. 'Goodbye. You're terribly wise, and perhaps a tiny bit cynical and you're laughing at me, aren't you?'

Mr Chorlton shook his head.

'My dear,' he said, 'I promise you I'm not. I was thinking – shall I tell you what I was thinking?'

'Go on,' said Jane, at the door, 'I shan't mind.'

'*These Christs that die upon the barricades, God knows that I am with them, in some ways.*'

She laughed, and went out. We heard her furiously bang the car door. I thought I wouldn't like to be the members of the Syndicate, whoever they were. Mr Chorlton said to me: 'I hope they don't offer her a cocktail. It'd be such an anticlimax.' But I felt sure they wouldn't. They wouldn't dare to. You couldn't offer a gin-and-bitters to an avenging angel.

The Purge for Poetry

Meanwhile Billy Butcher had been sitting alone in the corner and drinking whiskies almost as fast as Mrs Trentfield could serve them. He was long past the clowning stage – I dare say the Elmbury pubs had seen something of that, during the afternoon – and he looked terribly ill. I went across to him and asked him if he felt all right. He blinked and grinned.

'In the bag,' he said. 'It's in the bag.'

'*You're* in the bag.'

'Yes. Three bags full. Black sheep, black sheep, that's me. One for the somebody and one for the something and one for the little boy who lives in the lane. Mrs Trentfield! Please! One for the little boy who lives in the lane.'

'You've had enough, Master Billy,' she said.

'One for the little boy who lives in the lane.'

She poured him out a small one; but he was watching, and he shook his head. 'Double! Double, double, toil and trouble. How right those witches were!'

'Billy,' I said, 'you are a BF.'

'Many do call me a fool,' said Billy, almost startling me because I had so often thought of him as clowning like Andrew Aguecheek.

'That foolish knight,' said Billy, 'had a vacuum inside him.' He got up unsteadily and staggered to the bar, where Briggs, Sir Gerald, and Mr Chorlton were listening to another of Sammy's stories which I recognized immediately as the one about the geisha girl. Alfie and Joe had taken Rexy into the back room, where they waited for the vet.

Billy leaned against the bar and waved his glass in the air. He looked terrible. His eyes were red, his hair was falling over his forehead, and his features were becoming curiously blurred. In spite of his years of drinking Billy had a fine face; it was a face which even had a sort of nobility, but tonight the whisky had begun to rub out the nobility as moss and erosion and weathering Time will blur the crumbling features of a piece of sculpture. He was approaching the last stages of his bout; he'd blow up soon; and whether the eruption would be one of poetry or of window-breaking was simply a matter of chance.

'The foolish knight,' he repeated ' – I am not referring to you, Sir Gerald – had a vacuum inside him. But I am different. I am full. Full of whisky, and also of devils. Did you know that, Chorlton? I am possessed by devils.'

'I think we are all aware of it,' said Mr Chorlton.

'But they are no ordinary devils,' Billy went on with terrible seriousness. (It would be poetry and not windows, I thought with relief.) 'Their names are Ideas, Philosophies, unattainable Dreams, tormenting Thoughts, unwritten Epics, Sonnets, Songs, Ballads and Balderdash. If they were cast out into a herd of Gadarene swine the poor pigs would certainly run mad.'

' . . . These geisha girls,' said Sammy indomitably, 'they dance, you know, and they make you cups of tea. Don't you think, Billy, it's time you went home?'

Billy laughed.

'And a Voice valedictory, Who is for Victory? Who is for

Liberty? Who goes home? There I go, you see: the devils are stirring. But I deal with them as if I were a lion-tamer, though they are much more dangerous than lions. I command them: Down, sir, down, Ponto, down – Give me another drink, Mrs Trentfield – with a host of furious fancies whereof I am commander: that's me. Well, down the hatch boys. Down, Ponto, down.'

'Do shut up, Billy,' said Sammy Hunt. 'As I was saying, to cut a long story very short, these girls—'

'My trouble,' announced Billy in a loud voice, as if he were bearing witness to a sudden revelation, 'is that I am a sort of bottle.'

We all laughed at that.

'There's many a true word spoke in jest,' said Briggs.

Billy fixed us with a fierce and reproving look.

'You may laugh,' he said earnestly. 'I am a bottle, but not in the vulgar sense you mean. When I was a boy I was in the habit of swallowing poetry. In West Africa, where I was all alone in the jungle with a dusky lady and half a dozen books I swallowed a lot more. A terrible lot: Shakespeare, Marlowe, Donne, Keats, Swinburne. Then one day I put the cork in it; because it was bad for me, see, it was making me think. I put the cork in and took to whisky. No more poetry, I said; and except for the racing tips I haven't read a word since. But like parsnip wine when you bottle it too soon, it goes on working. This Skimble-Skamble stuff – who said that? I've forgotten – it fizzes inside me, and it's trying to blow out the bloody cork.'

Billy swayed and held on to the counter.

'Give me a whisky,' he said.

'No,' Mrs Trentfield had decided to be firm at last. 'You're not well, Master Billy. It would do you no good.'

'Presumptuous woman,' said Billy severely, 'how do you know? Are you a physician of the mind? Can you prescribe for my cerebellum? Whisky stops me thinking. Poetry makes me think. Thinking is disastrous. Ergo, whisky good, poetry bad. But nobody classifies Shakespeare as a Dangerous Drug. You don't have to get a licence to sell Swinburne. Suppose I ask you, Mrs Trentfield, for a half-pint of Housman? Ha ha! But it hurts, it torments, it keeps you awake, it gives you bad dreams; your whisky is harmless by comparison. Poetry is a curse, alcohol is a blessing. With a trifle of help from Mr Coleridge I made up a rhyme about alcohol the other day. Would you care to hear it? It goes like this:

> 'In Xanadu did Kubla Khan
> A sacred pleasure-drome decree
> Where Alc the sacred river ran
> Through taverns measureless to man
> Down to a sunless—

'Mrs Trentfield, I shall offend you if I go on. Give me another whisky. Give me one more.'

'Well, one small one and that's the last.' Mrs Trentfield poured it out reluctantly.

' "Come, cordial, and not poison, go with me," ' said Billy, and drank it. He was very near the edge now, I thought; this last one would topple him over. He suddenly fell silent; and Sammy, seizing his opportunity, began again:

'These girls are specially trained, you see, for the purpose of entertaining gentlemen—'

Billy cried angrily:

' "This is no world to play with mammets and to tilt with lips." Christ Almighty, what a world! "How weary, stale, flat and unprofitable seem to me all the uses of this world. 'Tis an unweeded garden, that's gone to seed." Like me. Gone to seed. Bloody well gone to seed at thirty-five.

"Methinks I have out-lived myself and grown to be a-weary of the sun. I have shaken hands with delight." You don't know who wrote that. None of you know. It came out of the bottle.'

'A vintage,' said Mr Chorlton, 'called Sir Thomas Browne.'

'I don't know, I've forgotten. But it came out of the bottle, the deadly dangerous bottle of stuff that makes you think.' Billy put his head in his hands. 'If man were drunk for ever,' he muttered. 'Half a pint of Housman. Christ, what a drink!' He looked up and quoted savagely:

> ' "But men at whiles are sober
> And think by fits and starts—"

'There you see: just what I've been saying. Listen, you fools, listen:

> "And when they think, they fasten
> Their hands upon their hearts."

'Oh, God, I can't bear it,' he cried. We recognized the symptoms; and sure enough, already the tears were rolling down his cheeks and his broad shoulders were heaving. Mrs Trentfield had her arm round his shoulder and began to lead him through the bar.

'It's all right, Master Billy, all you want is a bit of a lie-down, see, a quiet lie-down in the spare bedroom till you feel better . . .'

The Flood

After that I played a game of darts with Banks, while Sammy's familiar tale flowed majestically on towards its tantalizing climax (his ship's siren was hooting for him, the Japanese girl had her arms round his neck, If you leave me, she said, I shall commit hara-kiri). Then I heard the telephone ringing, and a moment later Joe came out of his back-room and said: 'That was the Colonel. He wants a bit of help. He says the flood's come up over the Summer Leasow and trapped his cattle and sheep. I told him we'd all be down there in a few minutes.'

Mrs Trentfield came bustling out with Joe's mackintosh. 'We do see Life,' she said.

We all packed into my little car, and I drove down the muddy lane which led towards the Lock. The ditches on either side of the lane were brimful, and in places were already overflowing. The Summer Leasow was a forty-acre meadow which lay in the bend of the river just past Sammy's cottage; it was a hayfield in summer and in autumn the Colonel pastured his Ayrshires, and a few of his queer Spanish sheep, upon the rich lattermath.

Before we got to Sammy's cottage we were driving axle-deep through flood-water which flowed like a little river between the hedges. The rain had stopped, and a half-moon was showing through torn and ragged clouds. By its light we could see ahead of us a muddy lake which was the Summer Leasow. 'Must be three feet of water there,' said Sammy. His cottage, which stood upon a bank, was well out of flood's way, but part of his garden was submerged and his boats, which he'd pulled up on the bank for tarring and winter repairs, were afloat already and tugging at their chains. 'Lucky I pegged 'em down,' he said. 'Otherwise they'd have been halfway to Elmbury. Maybe they'll come in useful.'

Now we could see lights moving over the Summer Leasow and their stippled yellow reflections in the water. We left the car and waded towards the gate; the bitter

cold water came up to our knees. When we reached the
gate we saw five figures about fifty yards away. We shouted
and they came slowly towards us. They carried torches
and hurricane lanterns, which showed up the bright
surge of the water round their legs as they pushed through
it. As they approached I recognized the Colonel and his
cowman. The Colonel was wearing his fishing-waders,
which came up to his waist, and in the light of his hurricane
lantern he looked more wonderfully grotesque than ever;
he looked like a kelpie emerging from his native lake. He
was swearing hard, and the sound came to us on the wind
like a deep purring growl.

'Here we are,' we shouted. 'What can we do to help?'

In shallower water now, he splashed more quickly
towards us. I noticed that he was carrying a shepherd's
crook. He said:

'We got most of the cows out; but there are two stuck in
the far hedge, and there's my goddam bull splashing about
somewhere and bellowing like hell. And there are six
sheep standing on that little tump of hay by the bank of
the river. Can't reach the sods except by swimming.'

'I'll go and fetch 'em in a punt,' said Sammy.

'How many are there of you?' called the Colonel.

I looked round, and was surprised to see that our
number was increased by more than a dozen. Alfie and
Dai Roberts had arrived carrying ropes, Jim Hartley from
the Adam and Eve, David Groves the ganger, the Rector,
two or three village boys, and even a few gipsyish figures,
unmistakable as Fitchers and Gormleys who always seemed
to appear magically in the village in moments of crisis. I
noticed that the three men standing in the shallow water
behind the Colonel were Pistol, Bardolph and Nym, and I
remembered that they had been picking sprouts for him;
but I should not have been at all surprised if they had

bicycled out from Elmbury, anticipating the flood, for
they too delighted in crises, which gave them wonderful
opportunities for scrounging, thieving, or earning tips.

'Well, Jim,' said the Colonel to Mr Hartley, 'I note that
thee turns out a lot quicker to a flood than to a fire! Or
hast'a brought thy old leaky pump to pump the river dry?'
He fell easily and without affectation into our country speech;
it came naturally to him; it wasn't part of a pose as it is
with some of our petty squires; he was genuinely bilingual.

Sammy said:

'We'll take four boats round by the river. Two of 'em
can take off the sheep and the other two can help you to
chivvy the cows and the bull.'

A few minutes later I found myself pulling one of
Sammy's row-boats down the channel between his osier-
beds. Sammy and Abraham the ferryman took the long
black punts, and Joe Trentfield followed me in a fourteen-
foot dingy. Sammy had provided each of us with ropes,
neatly coiled, and we each had a passenger armed with a
boathook. Mine was a murderous looking Fitcher or
Gormley who seemed extremely unhappy, having, perhaps,
some atavistic disquiet about boats and ropes and floods
and midnight adventuring upon the river.

As soon as we got out of the channel and into the main
stream I felt the strength of the flood. The current gave
a sharp tug at the stern and pulled the boat round so that
I lost ten yards before I began to make headway. Ahead of
me I could see Sammy and Abraham standing up in their
punts as they paddled them; Joe passed me with a couple
of strong pulls. What watermen the people of Brensham
were! They could all swim like otters from childhood and
they could handle any sort of boat with the skill and confidence of longshoremen. I thought: but they are hillmen too,
they walk like hillmen, and they're as happy on horse-back

as they are on the river; and they plough and dig and grow better sprouts than anybody else in the district! And they hang together, I thought, as Pistol once said. I felt proud to be with them and to belong to them, and I pulled hard at the sculls and got some way on the boat at last, so that I came level with Joe and saw over my shoulder the rhythmic dip of Sammy's paddle as he drove the long punt round the bend.

The horned Spanish sheep were jumping about and playing king of the castle upon the isolated hay-tump; they looked rather like ibex. Sammy shouted to me: 'They're too big for your boats. Abraham and I will take 'em off in the punts. You and Joe go hard a-starboard and help chivvy the old bull.' I swung my boat round the hay-tump and watched Sammy with two huge strokes bring his punt beautifully alongside it; then standing on the seat and looking like a giant against the moon he seized a struggling sheep and lowered it into the stern. Abraham's punt as black as Charon's nosed in beside his. I gave two hard pulls and felt the grip of the current suddenly loosen; it plucked feebly at the stern and then suddenly the boat shot ahead into the yellowish-brown backwater of the Summer Leasow.

I looked over my shoulder and caught sight of the moving lights carried by the Colonel and his men; and as I rowed towards them the Fitcher, or Gormley, cried 'Listen!' and I heard shouts, splashes and furious bellowing ahead. There were cries of 'Head him off! Head him off!' and a moment later the Ayrshire bull appeared in front of us, swimming like a hippo towards the river. Joe came along with the dinghy, and together we approached the bull until we were close enough to see his great flat head and the short curls between his horns. Then with an angry snort he turned, and we drove him back towards the shal-

lower water, rowing alongside him and prodding him now
and then with the boathook.

There was a gateway at the top of the meadow, the side
nearest to the Colonel's farm, and the men in the water
were herding two cows towards it; we drove the bull in the
same direction. Soon he joined the cows and with boats
and men forming a half-moon behind them they plunged
on through three feet of water towards the gap.

The approach to the gateway, of course, was deep and
muddy; we should have to swim them through it; but the
Colonel somehow or other had managed to open the gate
and he was now perched on top of it, swearing, waving,
and shouting instructions. The cows went through quietly
enough, but the bull took fright at the Colonel, who was
certainly a most alarming figure, and in the course of his
passage through the gateway he charged the open gate.
The Colonel toppled backwards off it and disappeared
beneath the water.

We in the boats could move quicker than the men who
were wading; so we were first in the gateway and I was able
to rescue, just as it was sinking, the Colonel's remarkable
hat. (The barbs of several fish-hooks pricked my fingers as I
grabbed it out of the water.) At first we could find no trace
of the Colonel himself; but Joe spotted two hands clutching
the middle bar of the gate and a moment later a grey
head appeared, and then an apologetic red face and a pair
of shoulders – this was indeed a kelpie rising from his
native deeps! – and we caught hold of the two hands and
tried to lift the Colonel out.

He was snorting exactly like his bull.

'You'll have to heave hard,' he spluttered. 'I seem to be
stuck in a sort of pismire.'

At last we got him into my boat. He looked pretty bad.
His teeth were chattering and his face was no longer

scarlet but bluish-grey. We laid him down between the seats and for a few moments he closed his eyes. I thought he had fainted; but his hand began to move feebly and patted the pocket of his jacket. His trembling fingers found the opening, the hand was inserted, and a moment later it brought out the flask. Immediately the Colonel opened his eyes and sat up. He unscrewed the top of the flask and began to drink. By some extraordinary chance it must have been full; for he was drinking for a good thirty seconds and we could hear the gulp and gurgle as the whisky went down. When the last drop was finished he wiped his moustache and the expression upon his face, which had been that of a dying grampus, suddenly changed. A thousand creases, puckers, and wrinkles appeared in his cheeks and round his eyes. 'Whisky inside and water out,' he grunted. He grinned. 'Do you know what happened?' he said. 'I fell in head first and my waders were filled with wind; so there I was like a bloody duck with me head in the muck and me arse in the air and floating round and round like a teetotum. I swear I must have swallowed half a dozen fishes!' – and then he threw back his head and began to laugh so loudly that even the men in the water, forty yards away, knew that he was still alive, so merrily that Pistol, Bardolph and Nym began to laugh too, a harsh cackle, a throaty guffaw, and a squeaky giggle respectively, borne to us across the swirling flood.

We Band of Brothers

In the Colonel's sitting-room, before a great log fire, we watched him slowly and steamily drying himself; for as usual he scorned to change his clothes and when Mr Chorlton prudently suggested that he should go to bed with

a hot water bottle he declared that he'd been to bed in
his time with a lot of peculiar things but never thank
God with that. He had invited us all back for drinks and
he had provided whisky, perry, home-made sloe gin,
parsnip wine, and two of his sister's famous caraway-seed
cakes. He drank most of the whisky himself, because, he
said, none of the other drinks would tolerate the amount of
dilution occasioned by the fact that his belly was half-full
of river water. Also, he declared, it would take something
pretty strong to kill the fishes which were swimming round
and round inside him.

There were at least twenty of us in the room, each
dripping our separate little pools upon the Colonel's carpet.
I was surprised to see Lord Orris and Jane, and even more
surprised to see Billy Butcher. He'd been sick, he whispered,
and the cold water had sobered him, and now he was
prepared to get drunk again on the Colonel's sloe gin. He
was said to have done great deeds in the water, having
actually swum twenty yards to release one of the cows which
was stuck in the hedge. 'Village drunk makes good,' he
said with a grin. 'Plucking bright honour from the pale-
fac'd moon.'

Each had his tale of adventure or mishap. Jane, who
feared bulls though probably she feared nothing else on
earth, had plunged into a blackthorn hedge, and torn her
skirt to ribbons, when the bellowing beast splashed towards
her. However, she still had a light of triumph in her eyes;
for she had paid her call upon the Syndicate, though she
would not tell us what she had said to them. 'It was an
extraordinary thing,' she said, 'but I got the impression
they were afraid of me.' I didn't think it was extraordinary
at all; what mortal would not be afraid when Pallas Athene
stood before him speaking winged words?

Lord Orris, ineffectual as ever, had succeeded in lassooing

a cow by the horns but had caught his own leg in the rope, so that he fell flat on his back in the water as soon as the cow plunged away. Sammy Hunt had been butted in the behind by the Spanish ram, which had nearly knocked him out of the punt. Sir Gerald Hope-Kingley had broken his spectacles, without which he was half blind, and Mr Mountjoy, misadventuring into a quagmire, had lost one of his shoes.

But incomparably the most perilous accidents had befallen Pistol, Bardolph and Nym. The bull, it seemed, had all but gored them in vulnerable and sensitive places; Bardolph, on one occasion had only escaped it by swimming underwater for twenty yards; Nym, on another, had actually leaped upon its back and steered it by the horns. The sheep, the cows and the bull would all have perished but for the courageous intervention of these three heroes. We listened to their tales in wonderment and admiration which was increased when we perceived that all three of them had managed to perform their aquatic feats without getting wet.

However, the Colonel gave them ten shillings each and being very full of perry they made a speech declaring that he was a gentleman for whom it would always be a pleasure to put themselves in mortal peril if the need should arise again. Then they took themselves off, and it was not until half an hour later, when the rest of the guests were leaving, that we missed three mackintoshes from the stand in the hall.

But they were old mackintoshes and their owners, who were Mr Chorlton, Billy Butcher, and Joe Trentfield, were mellowed by sloe gin so that they only laughed when Banks asked if they wanted him to take any action officially. 'Let the rogues have 'em,' said Mr Chorlton, 'for upon my soul I love a good rogue.'

The Colonel came to the door to see us off. The whisky

had warmed him, and his cheeks were as ruddy as autumn leaves. 'Thank you all,' he said. 'Thank you every one. But mind you, I expected no less when I rang up Joe. I knew I'd have half the village down at the Summer Leasow in ten minutes. For whatever they say about Brensham, we stick together, don't we?'

'Quite right, Colonel!' said Joe Trentfield. 'We may be a funny lot of beggars but we hangs together!'

So off we went down Magpie Lane, Joe and Alfie, David Groves and Dai Roberts, the Mad Lord with Jane beside him striding like a goddess, Jim Hartley waddling somewhat because he'd taken unusual exercise for a sluggish man, the Rector and Sir Gerald, Billy Butcher merry with sloe gin and reciting of all things 'Sohrab and Rustum' because the flooded river had reminded him of the Oxus, Sammy Hunt who'd tell in the years to come an unending tale of tonight's doings, some Fitchers and Gormleys walking in strict segregation, Mr Chorlton and I. And Mr Chorlton said: 'As Joe remarks, we're a curious lot of so-and-sos; but something binds us together, and although I've tried hard to find a definition for it, I'm blowed if I am able to put into words exactly what it is. Can *you* tell me?'

I shook my head.

'Sometimes,' said Mr Chorlton, 'I am inclined to think that it may be something very old and simple. I think it may be something to do with the Second Commandment.'

PART FOUR

THE FROST

*The Precocious Season – Whan that Aprille – The Halfway
People – The Home Orchard – Shourës Sote – Satyr and
Nymph – The Weathercock Turns North – The Reckoning –
The Aftermath – The Vultures Wait*

The Precocious Season

NEXT YEAR the spring came so early that not even the
longest memory could match its February celandines
and Lady-day cowslips. It came not shyly, as springs are
wont to do upon Brensham Hill, with a modest snowdrop in
the larch plantation, a self-effacing violet under the hedge;
but in triumph and sudden splendour 'with bows bent and
with emptying of quivers', with banners and trumpets,
with an army of crocuses and a fanfare of daffodils.

Even in February, when Alfie was spraying his plum
trees, there were blue days that rightly belonged to late
March. The rooks flew clamorous to their nests in the wine-
red elms, and Mr Mountjoy's bees emerged from their
hives in thousands and were rewarded for this act of faith
by the golden pollen upon the pussy-willows by the river.

Alfie finished spraying, and began to plough between his
lines of plum trees. He didn't plant anything there, but
performed the cultivation as a free gift to his orchards;

otherwise the rank-growing grass and weeds would suck the richness from the soil and starve the hungry trees. Very few of our fruit-growers took the trouble to do this; but Mr Chorlton pointed out that it was a very ancient cultivation, and when we asked him what he knew about agriculture, he told us with a smile: 'It is recommended in the Georgics, Book II.'*

March, robbed by February, stole in turn some sunshine, some flowers, and even some thrushes' nests from April; and so week by week the prodigal business went on of robbing Peter to pay Paul, and the old men complained that the seasons were out of joint and prophesied that Time would bring its revenges. By April Fools' Day the weeds stood high in the ditches, hedge-parsley made a pattern like old lace, and on the banks with celandines and violets the stitchwort unfolded its petals which were like new-laundered linen. There were white butterflies fluttering everywhere, Mr Chorlton had seen the first orange-tips and holly blues, and in Mr Mountjoy's rectory garden a precocious blackbird had already hatched her young.

Whan that Aprille

And of course, by April Fools' Day, the plum blossom was fully out in all the orchards along the vale; for every sprouting and blossoming thing was three weeks ahead of its normal season. Easter, as well as the spring, was early that year; and like an Easter bride Brensham was dressed in white.

It happened that I had been away from Elmbury and hadn't visited Brensham for several months. Certain things

* I looked it up and of course he is quite right. *Namque omne quotannis Terque quaterque solum scidendum glæbaque versis Aeternum fragenda bidentibus, omne levandum Fronde nemus.*

had occurred to me which are of no importance to this tale:
I had left my uncle's office in Elmbury and apprenticed
myself to a different trade, that of writing books. So I was
now free to live and work wherever I liked, and I had spent
most of the winter in London. With all the greater delight,
therefore, I saw Brensham in blossom when I walked over
its hill upon that first day of April.

I went up as far as the Folly and visited the ancient
eremite who had put on his straw hat with the I. Zingari
band in honour of the blue skies. He told me that in all his
years he had never seen so much blossom; and when I
looked down from the Folly roof I felt sure he must be right,
for the whole of the vale and the lower slopes of the hill were
buried beneath a vast snowdrift of petals. As a rule the
effect, as you look down upon the flowering vale, is that of a
lace curtain stretched loosely over it; for the plum blossoms
are very small and even though they be multitudinous the
leafless sepia twigs still show among them. However, in this
season of unparalleled prodigality I had the impression not
of a lace curtain but of foam and lather, of curds overflowing
from a dish of cream. 'Not once in fifty years,' said the
Hermit, 'have I gazed upon such a sight;' and in his eye
there was a look of pride and of possession: 'Mine, all
mine!'

Later in the day I went down into the village and met
Alfie, who took me into his orchards to see the flower-laden
boughs. He, too, said that he'd never seen anything like it.
If one blossom in twenty bore a plum, the branches would
break under the burden. We stood in the sunshine beneath
the myriad boughs in which the bees already were fertilizing
the flowers, and Alfie said:

'There's probably nothing in it, but they say you get a
good season every four years. Last year 'twas middling, the
previous year 'twas very middling, and the year before that

the plum-picking was like hunting for needles in haystacks. If we got a good crop this summer it'd square up a bit, and there'd be fewer of us getting nasty letters from the bank.'

'Well, this seems like fourth time lucky,' I said, glancing up at the boughs which looked as if they were draped in white chiffon.

'Seems like? Maybe. But 'tis too early for my liking,' said Alfie with a shrug. 'If it froze smartish tonight, we mightn't have so much as a bud left tomorrow. And there's six weeks to go yet before we're safe. I've known hailstorms and black frosses even in May.'

He walked with me to the gate. I said:

'It must be an anxious time, while you're waiting.'

He pointed to a small wet-and-dry thermometer which hung on the gatepost.

'It gives you the jim-jams,' he said. 'Every night at six o'clock I takes a look at that hygrometer. 'Tis a better indication to my mind than the barometer or the wireless. If it looks good I thank the Lord. If it looks tricky I prays.'

But tonight the two columns of mercury stood nearly level, and the temperature was fifty-one. There was a warm wet breeze from the south-west.

'All right for twenty-four hours,' said Alfie, and grinned.

The Halfway People

As I walked down the village street, where even in the cottage gardens were blossoming trees, two or three in a back-yard, two score in a little paddock, so that their whiteness spilled between the brown thatch, and the very village became an orchard, it occurred to me how precarious was the condition of the people of Brensham, whose little fortunes were bound to these frail and transient petals. To

Alfie and his kind a black frost might mean a loss of four or five hundred pounds; but to Jim Hartley with his single orchard adjoining the Adam and Eve the loss of one hundred would be severe in proportion, whereas to Mrs Doan, who had a dozen trees behind her shop, or to David Groves the ganger, whose small garden contained only four, a bad season might mean the foregoing of luxuries, the postponement of a holiday, or even the spending of precious savings. Impartial as death were the cold fingers of the frost when they groped their way through the village and along the vale; and from rich and poor alike they took all.

I thought: perhaps after all the people of Brensham are different from other folk; for they experience each year this brief and terrible loveliness, which makes them poets, and yet know each year this sense of terrible transience, which makes them philosophers. They are a halfway people, I thought; they dwell halfway between the hill and the river, holding allegiance to both, and halfway between beauty and ugliness, looking out alternately upon slummy sproutfields and exquisite blossom. And for the whole of their short season of breath-taking beauty, they are poised halfway between triumph and disaster while the weather spins its age-old wheel, and the cold croupier Frost stands by in readiness to sweep the stakes towards him.

But tonight, while the wheel still spun, the soft southerly breeze held steady, and brought with it a few warm raindrops and a few spent petals from early trees already overblown. All was well so far; and Brensham held its breath.

The Home Orchard

April passed like a cheerful debtor, spendthrift of its days borrowed from May. By day the sun shone and the sap rose in the trees; Mr Mountjoy's four million bees were kept busy all day vicariously consummating a myriad marriages between flower and flower; by night showers as soft as the bees' kiss refreshed the blossoms, and winds as light as a sigh bore away the unwanted petals when the fruit began to form.

Mr Chorlton brewed his treacly intoxicant and began his nocturnal mothing earlier in the season than ever before. Sammy Hunt painted his boats in anticipation of Whitsun visitors. Mrs Hartley spring-cleaned the Adam and Eve in case any obstinate motes had withstood her twice-daily dustings. Sir Gerald planted out – rare titbits for the slugs! – some valuable Alpines he had obtained from Tibet. Only too aware of the sword over its head, Brensham nevertheless rejoiced in the sunshine and busied itself with the duties and pleasures of the spring.

Jane Orris, her adventurous spirit made more restless by the season, brought an aeroplane to Brensham; the same benevolent aunt, no doubt, who paid her fees at Oxford had provided the money it cost her to learn to fly. The Moth, which she landed rather dangerously in the long flat field below the Manor, was painted bright red and shining silver and it looked like a giant toy. Almost every morning Jane took off over the crooked chimneys of the House Narrow and performed her tyro loops over the church spire and brought the villagers into the street when she dived upon the Adam and Eve.

Once or twice I met her, in the pubs or walking on the hill. She was lovelier than ever; she wore the spring like a new frock and in her eyes was that mystical and trans-cendent look which belongs to those who discover for the first time the bright-shining regions above the clouds.

I asked her: 'Jane, how did you get it? Did your aunt buy it for your twenty-first birthday present?'

She laughed and shook her head.

'Hire purchase,' she said. 'I managed to borrow just enough for the first three payments. You see, I look upon it as a sort of investment.'

'An investment?' There was a terrible lot of old Orris in Jane.

'Yes. I thought I'd fly it to America or Australia or some-where and restore the family fortunes,' she said airily.

'Like Amy Johnson?'

'Yes. Only I suppose I'll have to go farther or faster or something. At present I'm only practising cross-countries. I can't even do a proper slow-roll.'

'You needn't do slow-rolls all the way to Australia.'

'I suppose not. I always think I'm going to fall out. But listen,' she said, suddenly serious. 'The family fortunes will have to be restored, and pretty quick too. As you know, Father borrowed money from the Syndicate, on a mortgage, and then he borrowed some more, and if he can't pay the interest in the autumn, I think they'll pounce. The fruit might just save us.'

'That big orchard at the bottom of the drive?'

'Yes, the Home Orchard. Come and see it!' she begged. 'The trees are old, and half of them are falling down, but I've never seen such blossom. I'll show you a chaffinch nest on an apple bough if you'll come.'

She led me down the hill by the same rough scrambling way she had shown us when she was a small girl. I said: 'Jane, do you remember how you took us down into the vault to see your crusader in his urn? Is he still there? – for I had heard tales of a winter flood which had filled the vault with four feet of water and even burst open the coffins, so that when it subsided the bones and skulls of previous lords and ladies Orris littered the muddy floor in sacrilegious and incestuous confusion. Jane laughed. 'Yes, I rescued Robert;

though he was very nearly drowned. And we got Mr Mountjoy to bury the others in the churchyard, though I'm afraid we muddled them up a bit, putting them back in their boxes.'

'What did you do with your crusader?' I asked.

'I keep him in my bedroom! It sounds gruesome, but his urn is so lovely, you know. Thou still-unravished bride of Quietness, and of course one doesn't look inside.'

As we came down into the Park I noticed that the spire of the private chapel had fallen through the roof. There was ruin everywhere, the wind blew through gaping holes in stable and shedding, and at least another dozen of the Manor's top-storey windows were patched with brown paper so that the house looked more than ever like a blinded Argus.

'Isn't it awful?' said Jane. 'But never mind: when I make my Record Flight and win a lot of money we'll patch it up!'

I thought they'd have to be quick about it, or the whole house would fall down. We picked our way through the boggy kitchen-garden, which grew little for the kitchen and was a garden only in name. Today it was ablaze with marsh-marigolds growing where the cabbages should have been. Four rabbits jumped up under our feet and ran away through a hole in the tangled wire-netting. Jane remarked with a sort of sorrowful pride:

'Perhaps ours is the only house in the whole world which has kingcups growing in the back-garden.'

We came to the Moat, where a rare and lovely fern called Osmunda grew upon the bank and gave to Lord Orris his only fame; for if you look up 'Brensham' in the guidebook you will find under Orris Manor this single sentence:

'Seat of Lord Orris and notable for a remarkable growth of the rare fern *Osmunda regalis* on the banks of the Moat.'

But now even the Osmunda seemed to be sharing in the general decay; the flood had washed the soil from its roots, and only a few fronds were sprouting among the withered brown ones.

'Botanists used to come hundreds of miles to see it,' said Jane regretfully. 'Father used to run away from them: he thought they were duns.'

We crossed the Moat by a shaky wooden bridge from which several planks were missing. The stagnant water was green and smelly, and upon it lived a single Muscovy duck in mournful solitude. He was the last of a collection of Ornamental Waterfowl which Lord Orris had prodigally purchased in more prosperous days. ('We ate all the others,' said Jane.) His wings had been clipped so that he could not fly; this indignity, or perhaps his lack of a mate, or perhaps merely an innate and incurable melancholy like Jacques', caused him to wear an appearance of utter dejection. He croaked without ceasing a plaintive and self-pitying soliloquy. Jane said:

'He must be very old. I invented a rhyme about him when I was a child:

> ' *The Muscovy duck*
> *Goes cluck, cluck, cluck.*'

He was still going cluck this morning, railing dismally against the world. The scum lay thick on the surface of the water and as he swam it piled up in front of his breast like dirty cream. He had much to complain of. Cluck, cluck, cluck, he said. It was his protest against scum, against exile, against solitude, against everything.

We went down the mossy unrutted drive, scarred only by the half-moons of Rosinante's shoes, and suddenly the Home Orchard lay before us, clothed in such surpassing beauty that it astonished me, for I had thought it shared the ruin which seemed to be the common lot of all the Mad Lord's possessions. I had seen it in late autumn, when the old trees were sooty-black with pale streaks of lichen like horrible sores, gibbous like ancient crones, their backs bent with the burden of the years, boughs like skeleton arms, twigs like crooked fingers pointed earthwards in despair or to the sky in supplication. Some were split in two, cleft by frost or lightning, some leaned drunkenly, some, half-uprooted, were locked together by their leprous branches in a macabre embrace. Their few yellowing leaves fluttered with a sort of nihilistic impatience as if they begged the winds, Take me and do your will.

But now! – the graveyard had blossomed, it was Resurrection Morning, the white and the green and the shell-pink so smothered the trees that you could scarcely see the sooty trunks. And all the birds in Brensham, surely, were singing among the young crisp leaves.

'Now I'll show you my chaffinch nest,' said Jane. 'But first: isn't it unbelievably lovely? I have a silly fancy about it. I'll tell you. It happens to be the only piece left which Father hasn't borrowed money on. It's still ours: all of it, trees and grass and earth. So I says to myself, That's why, of course! The Syndicate hasn't got its dirty fingers on it!'

She laughed. 'Once, years ago,' she went on, 'we sold the fruit in it for four hundred and fifty. Perhaps we shall again. That would save us for another year.'

'I hope so,' I said. 'My dear, I hope so.'

'Well, you never know.' She looked suddenly serious. 'It's Nathan's ewe-lamb, anyhow. It's Naboth's vineyard. It's all we've got.'

Shourës Sote

It was then about the middle of April. The improbable
weather continued without a break. Blue days alternated
with dappled ones; and whenever the springing grass grew
thirsty a dove-grey cloud would sprinkle a blessing upon it
and then swiftly pass as if it were aware that it intruded.
Surely there had never before been such a spring! Never
before a cobalt mist of bluebells in Orris' coverts before the
cuckoos came; never before in the Summer Leasow a
carpet of buttercups to welcome the swallow. The prodigal
and reckless season had its effect upon us all, so that Mimi
Trentfield came out in the most ridiculous hats and Meg
fell hopelessly in love with a photograph of Clark Gable.
The Colonel sold his motor-cycle and bought an old car,
which he drove even more dangerously. Mr Chorlton and
Briggs worked harder than ever to put the cricket-pitch in
order for the first match, and argued more fiercely so that
the inhabitants of Magpie Lane, hearing their shouts, often
feared lest they should come to blows. Mr Mountjoy was
seen to go fishing in his biretta, scandalizing his church-
wardens, and even Dai Roberts' puritanism melted before
the warm wantonness of Nature and he confessed to me
when I met him one day that he was engaged upon a poem
of forty pennillion and that for the first time in his career as
a poet the subject was Profane.

'And what is it?' I asked.

Dai blushed.

'It iss my wife Mary,' he said.

The admission, it seemed, embarrassed him; for he
climbed up on his bone-shaking bicycle and began to ride
away. He was as thin as a rake, and indeed had been nick-
named by Mr Chorlton Praisegod Barebones. His wife, in

contrast, had a soft and pleasing plumpness; and the recol-
lection of this, or perhaps some stray lines of his new poem
still buzzing in his head, must have prompted the remark
which he made to me over his shoulder as he went down the
lane.

'Rough and steep iss the road,' he said, 'and hard and
lumpy is the saddle, and I have less flesh on my bones than
I used to. I wish,' he added with earnest regret — 'I often
wish that I had the bottom of Mary!'

Satyr and Nymph

Something worse than a mere spring-fever had affected Mrs
Doan's daughter, young Sally. She moped and she drooped
like those primroses on the hill whose brief season was
already done: 'a malady most incident to maids'. What I
had guessed at the Woody Bourton cricket-match I now
knew for sure, and if I needed confirmation I had it from
Billy Butcher himself. He had endured for many weeks a
spell of haggard sobriety. We knew it could not last and sure
enough he went off to Elmbury one market day and I found
him in the Swan at ten o'clock in the evening, sitting alone
and helpless in a corner of the bar, having missed the last
train and the last bus and even that later bus, the Colonel's
old car, which often brought late revellers back from Elmbury
to Brensham. He was in a bad way, having achieved the
painful condition of tottering and tearful drunkenness
which we knew as his Poetic Stage. So I took him home,
and had to listen to one of those curious outpourings which
seemed to flow straight from his subconscious when the
whisky broke down the dams.

'What,' he demanded, 'is the use of a man who is a mere
bottle? A pint, a magnum, a demijohn, a jeroboam full of

undigested poetry? A flask, a flagon, a fiasco – my God, yes
– a fiasco indeed! A pitcher broken at the cistern – a
calabash, an old leaky calabash like they had in West
Africa where I lived with a dusky lady. Did I ever tell you
that? Where she lives it's dark and shady. Put my money
on Sally Brown. Ha, ha! Put my money on Sally Doan!'

He laughed and fell silent. Then he said suddenly:

'What would you say if I married her?'

I didn't know what to say. I improvised:

'I'd think she'd taken on a bit of a handful, Billy.'

'How right you are! Come live with me and be my love,
And we will all the pleasures prove of living with a drink-
sodden half-demented battered broken sot who stinks of
stale whisky. No! A thousand times no! I put her out of my
mind. I dismiss the thought. Sally is gone that was so kindly,
Sally is gone from Hannaker Mill.'

He coughed, and muttered something else which I could
not hear; and a moment later when I glanced at him I
noticed that he was asleep. In the dim light of the dashboard
lamp his lean tormented face looked very like a satyr's; and
yet, I thought, this time it was the nymph who pursued
and the satyr who ran away. I hoped devoutly, for his own
sake and Sally's, that he'd keep on running.

The Weathercock Turns North

May came in with sunshine as hot as June's, and Alfie sent
his old ladders to be mended, for he'd need all he had at
picking-time if the crop was as good as it promised to be.
The fruit had set already and the petals had blown away;
on every small twig you could count a score of the small
green berry-like plums.

The great apple tree which stood beside the Horse

Narrow was already showering its petals on the front door-step, and its leafy branches in front of the windows made a cool green shade inside the bar. A positive choir of birds seemed to have their homes in it, so that as you drank your beer you were serenaded by a perpetual twittering and chirruping and merry fluting. Mr Chorlton was reminded of a favourite quotation from Euripides: 'The apple tree, the singing and the gold.' 'You've got the first two,' he said to Joe, 'and you'll have the gold when you sell all those Blenheims at five bob a pot.'

But on May the third, though the sky remained blue, there was a slight and subtle change in the weather. It was still hot enough to make you sweat if you dug in your garden or climbed the hill; but the breeze was cooler and the air felt curiously dry. We had a cricket-practice in the evening and the Colonel came down to watch us. He'd been shooting magpies and carrion-crows, his favourite pastime at this season when there were very few other creatures which might lawfully be killed, and he still carried his gun under his arm: 'Thought I'd wait under the willows to see if I could get a pigeon,' he said. Pigeons also were fair game in May.

I waited with him for half an hour, and then he took me down to the Summer Leasow to see his heron's nest. The nearest heronry was up-river, twelve miles away; but this spring a single pair had come to the Summer Leasow and built their nest in one of the tall elms. Nothing could have given the Colonel greater pleasure; and he from whose sharp old eyes and deadly gun no bird of the air was safe now declared fiercely that he would shoot anybody he caught interfering with his herons. I think he felt they had done him a signal honour by coming to nest on his land; they had put themselves under his protection. 'They might have gone to old Orris,' he said, 'or to the Syndicate, whose keepers would have polished 'em off in no time. How marvellous that they should come to *me*! I swear I'll pepper the first bird's nesting brat who so much as glances up at those elms! What an *annus mirabilis* this is! It's my seventieth, and it looks like being the best fruit year I've ever known—' He broke off abruptly, paused, and sniffed the air like a dog. Suddenly he said:

'It's going to freeze.'

'What, in May? Can you smell it?'

'I don't know if I smell it or simply feel it in my bones,' he said, 'but it's going to freeze smartish and I'm frightened for the plums.'

The Colonel always felt the weather in his bones. I never knew what he meant by this phrase, but I think it had nothing to do with the aches and pains and sharp twinges by which old people are apt to prognosticate the rain or the cold. It was something more profound than that; he meant that he was aware of coming changes as the trees in their sap feel them, as the grass at its tangled roots or the chrysalis deep in the ground feels them, as the very earth feels them, for he was nearer to these things than other men, there was something Protean about him.

When I passed through the village on my way home I glanced at the gilded weathercock on top of the church spire; and sure enough it was beginning to swing through west to the northward, the wind had started to veer. I called on Alfie and had a look at his hygrometer. The column from the dry bulb had climbed high above the wet one showing that the air was exceptionally dry. The barometer was rising too, said Alfie. He didn't much like the look of it; but the chances of a really damaging frost so late in the season weren't very high and he said with a grin:

'If old Jack Frost takes one fruit in five, he can have 'em and welcome. They'll do with a bit of thinning. They'll bust the trees else.'

The Reckoning

The frost was sharpish but although it whitened the lawns and laid a smear of cat-ice on the ponds and even made the flowers droop their heads for a few hours after dawn, it did small harm to the well-formed fruit. The morning broke blue and the sun soon warmed the chilly ground. Then, in the early afternoon, the wind rose and a long black cloud with ragged edges appeared in the sky. A sudden brief hailstorm swept along the vale. It lasted only ten minutes, but just before dusk there came another, which lashed the leafy boughs of the trees and passed with a high shrill wind that knew nothing of summer. The three months' chicanery, the borrowing from Peter to pay Paul, had come to an end at last. That night brought the reckoning.

Measured in degrees Fahrenheit, on Alfie's thermometer, the reckoning was sixteen degrees; sixteen degrees of black blighting blistering frost.

He told me afterwards that although he went out into his orchards soon after dawn, and walked between the rows of trees for nearly an hour, he did not at first realize the extent of the calamity. It took a hefty clout to break the ice on the duck-pond, but there was no hoar frost on the grass or the hedges, and as the sun rose in the pale sky Alfie examined the small green glistening plums (they were about the size of hawthorn berries), and tried to persuade himself that they had come to no harm.

'I went home and had my breakfast and the Missus said, "Alfie, the redcurrants are done, and the lettuces are black, and the hollyhocks are cut down as if someone had slashed them with a stick. There's nothing left in the garden at all."'

So Alfie went back to his orchards and now that the sun

had warmed the trees and made the sap run again the huge
catastrophe was suddenly apparent. Alfie could see the
bunches of little plums hanging black and blasted upon the
twigs; here and there were a few green ones, but when he
pulled off a sample dozen and opened them with his finger-
nail he discovered that every one was going black inside.
Even the young leaves at the twig-ends drooped, brown and
withered already as if a pack of mischievous children had
run from tree to tree tweaking them.

Still Alfie couldn't believe that the destruction was
complete and absolute. He ran about his land in panic, he
told us afterwards with his familiar grin, trying to find some
sheltered or shady place which the groping fingers of the
frost had failed to reach. But there was none; and last of all
he went to his strawberry bed, which he had covered the
night before, and took off the straw, and began to pull open
the tight-green flower-buds. Almost every one was brown and
shrivelled. There was nothing left anywhere, nothing at all.

At noon Alfie went down to the Horse Narrow. It was
unusually full, for nobody felt much like working and in any
case the Horse Narrow was a sort of village club in which
men tended to gather at times of crisis. Several of the fruit-
growers had brought with them grisly exhibits; twigs of
plum, apple and cherry upon which, as upon Alfie's, every
little embryo was spoiled. Some of these twigs bore a greater
number of berries than anybody could remember having
seen before; Sammy Hunt counted seventy-three on a
branch only fifteen inches long. (That would be something
to remember, something to tell a tale about in after years!)
Even as the branch lay upon Joe Trentfield's counter every
berry withered and went brown. Somebody pointed out a
small green caterpillar crawling sluggishly among the
leaves. 'Still alive! The frost killed the plums, but it didn't
kill 'ee!' Alfie grinned. 'I reckon he's welcome to what he

can get, now; there's nowt left that matters to us, on any of the trees.'

Joe had an exhibit of his own. 'Come and look at my garden,' he said. Mrs Trentfield served teas in the garden to summer visitors, and Joe had planted a large number of geraniums, stocks, and tulips 'to make the place look cheerful'. Now Joe, as we have seen, was remarkably casual, haphazard, and happy-go-lucky in his conduct of the business and in his dealings with his customers. His gloriously untidy bar was Liberty Hall. But in his gardening, and only in his gardening, the Regimental Sergeant-Major appeared. His flowerbeds were laid out like a barrack square; and Joe couldn't abide the slightest irregularity in the rows nor any sign of indiscipline among their occupants. If any plant showed a tendency towards individuality or waywardness he ruthlessly cut it back. Intruders upon the parade ground he fell upon as if they had been defaulters. The flowers in his garden must always be dressed by the right, numbered, sized, proved and properly covered off. 'No talking in the rear rank!' you could imagine Joe telling them.

This morning, in consequence, Joe's garden presented an astonishing sight. The black frost's sabre had mown down all the rows with neatness and symmetry. A regiment of tulips had kept their dressing even as they fell; two companies of stocks, having formed square had fallen in that same formation, displaying the discipline of Guards; a platoon of geraniums still held their ground and gallantly remained standing though the blackened head of each one drooped as if the scimitar had passed with deadly precision along their unwavering line.

'All that work for nothing!' said Joe. 'The work of weeks destroyed in a night!'

'Ah well,' said Alfie with a grin. 'They died with their boots clean, Joe.'

Back in the bar Joe bought a round of drinks; and Sammy Hunt began to tell a story which no one had heard before, concerning a frost of remarkable severity he had endured in Alaska. This was unfamiliar territory to Sammy's listeners; and some wondered, though none dared to ask, what brought his tramp-steamer trading there. However, Sammy told his tale with great verisimilitude and as usual in minute detail.

'To cut a long story very, very short, we were getting hungry because the pemmican was frozen so solid that you could scarcely break it with a lumberman's axe; so we tried to cut a hole in the ice of the lake, to see if we could get some fish. Well, believe it or not, every time we dropped our lines in it froze up pronto, so that we couldn't pull the lines out and lost our precious hooks—'

Alfie interrupted the story to buy another round; then Briggs bought one, then Billy Butcher; for there was nothing to be done about the blasted orchards, and a catastrophe so profound deserved some sort of celebration. They drank grimly at first, as a beaten army drinks to its defeat; but soon they began to recollect as they stood around the bar the good seasons and the bad, the fat years that had made them rich, the lean ones that had nearly ruined them. They could laugh, now, about some of the disasters that had attended them in the past; and they knew, being market-gardeners and therefore philosophers, that some time hence they would be able to laugh at this one. 'Ten years ago,' mused Alfie, 'I built great bonfires all round my orchards; twenty quid it cost me, and I thought, now let the blessed frost come and I shall be the only man in the district with a crop worth picking. But there wasn't no frost that year, and there was so many plums that it wasn't worth sending them to market. I let my bonfires stand; and next year, as you'll recollect, there came a nasty frost one night at the end of

April. I sensed it coming. The wind was in the east; so I lit the bonfires on the east side of my orchards and went to bed. About midnight, when I was fast asleep, the wind changed; and it froze like billy-o from the north-west. I lost all my plums; and the only good my bonfires did was to save a tuppeny-hapenny patch of gooseberries in a garden on the other side of the road owned by an old bitch called Mrs Parsons who I hated. Very grateful was Mother Parsons' – Alfie grinned – 'next Christmas she sent me a very small bottle of green gooseberry wine.'

Each had his tale of great frosts in years long past. The Colonel told how in 1895 the severe weather lasted from January to the end of March: 'You could still feel the bone in the ground,' he said, 'when you came to get the soil ready for planting your peas and beans.' Briggs remembered a season when April snow had come simultaneously with April blossom, so that from the hilltop you could scarcely tell which was which. Sammy had a story of the song-thrush frozen to her nest in a 'silver thaw' at the end of March. Joe Trentfield called to mind old Jacob Grindley, 'the meanest, miserablest old miser as ever lived at Brensham', who was the first man in the district to own a wireless crystal-set and who therefore was able to get a later weather forecast than anybody else. He couldn't abide to think of his neighbours sharing this information free-gratis-and-for-nothing and if you met him in the evening and asked him: 'Is it going to freeze, Mr Grindley?' he'd tell you: 'I dunno. The wireless wouldn't work. I couldn't get anything out of it but squeaks and groans' – but ten minutes later you'd see him hurrying towards his strawberry-beds with a boltin of straw.

'I minds him doing that,' said Alfie. 'He saved his strawberries and I lost all my plums. Come to think of it, I'd just had my ladders mended that year too! Seems it's unlucky to mend your ladders till you sees the fruit on the trees!'

'Ah well, Alfie,' said the Colonel wisely, 'if there's anything Jack Frost teaches us it's this: 'tis no use looking up into the trees for your rent. Where you've got to get it from is down *here*' – he pointed with his stick at the ground— 'and what you get up top is just perks.'

'That's the way it is,' said Alfie with a shrug. It was nearly closing-time, and he made his way home, had his midday bait, and spent an hour or two tidying up the Missus' garden. Then he took his two sons out on to the land and went to work with a will in the hot sunshine which mocked the blasted trees; he set one of them to hoeing between the bean-rows, the other to skimming off a frosted crop of peas, and he himself began to plant out another batch of lettuces.

'For that's where your profits come from,' he told his boys. 'Out of the ground.'

The Aftermath

But not every man who owned an orchard or a few plum-trees was also a market-gardener. As Mr Chorlton drily put it, the trouble with most of the people of Brensham was that they had all their egg-plums in one basket. One season's dead loss might not indeed ruin them; but it meant hard times for all, especially as it came at a time of agricultural unemployment and trade depression.

As if to emphasize the mutability of human fortunes and the fond frailty of human hopes, the sun shone throughout the rest of May and the warm nights brought with them the merest zephyrs from the soft south. These infinitesimal winds, which faintly stirred the branches of apple and plum, were sufficient nevertheless to dislodge a steady shower of small brown withered berries. Obedient to Newton's Third Law, they fell with a gentle patter, as of summer rain, to the ground.

'Allegorical it iss,' said Dai Roberts Postman, 'for what are man's dreams but shrivelled husks when God in His wisdom iss moved to nip them in the bud?' And for many days he relieved the monotony of his round by composing an allegorical poem entitled 'The Chastisement of Nature Upon the Wanton Prodigality of her Children'.

This, however, was little comfort to Brensham. During the weeks following the frost the village like a broken army after battle learned of its casualties one by one. Alfie, it seemed, would be five hundred pounds down on his year's trading; for he had sprayed and he had ploughed, spent a lot of money on artificial manure, bought extra equipment and a new horse. Now he would have to borrow money from the bank and struggle hard to keep his head above water until next season. All the other market-gardeners were heavy losers, and the Colonel, whose farm included forty acres of orchard, was reputed in spite of his private means to be in a bad way. Lord Orris would almost certainly be unable to pay his mortgage interest when it became due; and even the cottages such as David Groves were hard hit, for many of them counted on their plums or apples for the money they needed to buy and feed the pig which they hoped to kill at Christmas.

It was the first summer in any man's memory during which not a single pot of plums left Brensham station; generally, at the peak of the season, the railway company ran a special train every night. Whereas a score of 'little men' would normally sell their fruit for, say, twenty-five or fifty pounds, and two-score owners of bigger orchards might get seventy or a hundred, this year nobody received a penny. The total loss ran into thousands; and that meant that Mrs Doan sold less groceries, the pubs sold less beer, and almost everybody in the village – and in Elmbury as well – was directly or indirectly affected. One of the first casualties was the poor little landlord of the Trumpet. He was sold up in August, and another optimist reigned in his stead.

To make matters worse there was a bad slump in onions, a crop which was another of Brensham's staples. Early in the season the market-gardeners had been offered as much as seventy pounds an acre. They refused the offer because they had plenty of labour to fork them up and bundle them and send them to market; they thought they'd make more that way, and they needed all they could make. But the day before the first batch was ready the foreign onions began to arrive and 'the bottom fell out of the market' suddenly. The price was 2½d a dozen bundles. When he heard the news Alfie went home and did a long complicated sum – he wasn't very good at sums, he frequently licked his blunt pencil and added up the figures several times but he was always right in the end – and when he had finished he discovered that it was *costing* him 2½d a dozen bundles to get the onions out of the ground.

So he grinned and shrugged his shoulders and ploughed in the crop which, a few weeks before, had been worth two hundred pounds.

'In times of scarcity,' he said, 'you're broke because you ain't got nowt to sell; in times of plenty you're broke because you can't sell what you've got. It's helluva puzzling!'

The Vultures Wait

I was away for most of the summer; and when I came back in September, and played in the last cricket-match of the season, I found the village still talking about the Great Frost. The shadow of the disaster remained upon Brensham. Lord Orris, I was told, stood nearer than ever before to bankruptcy; nevertheless he had refused to accept his Michaelmas rent from any man who relied wholly or partly on fruit for his living. All the tenants, well knowing his straits, had saved, stinted and even borrowed to pay him in full on the day of the Audit; but the Mad Lord, who employed no agent and who received his rent in person over a glass of cider in his chilly morning-room which the duns had ransacked until it was practically bare, had waved them away with a courteous gesture of refusal.

'My dear fellow, you will only embarrass me if you insist. The cruel frost robbed us all; but if I exacted from you a rental for which you have received nothing in return, I should be a robber too. I shall manage somehow, I assure you; my needs are very small. Next year, perhaps, you will all make a fortune: and I, who have done nothing to deserve it, will share in your good luck.'

They told me this story in the Horse Narrow, after cricket, where Sammy Hunt was still comparing Brensham's frost with that of Alaska.

'I'm not leg-pulling,' I heard him say, 'though you may find it difficult to believe me when I tell you that it was downright dangerous – on account of the risk of frost-bite – to attempt to obey the ordinary, trivial calls of nature—'

Alfie was in the pub, and Mr Chorlton, Briggs and Banks and David Groves; but there were very few of the labouring men, and those whom I saw were more inclined to drink half-pints of cider than pints of beer. Mr Chorlton told me that he had started what he called 'a small semi-private fund' to aid any cottager who might be unable to afford his usual Christmas pig. 'A sort of unofficial pig club,' he said. 'We provide feeding-stuffs on credit, and things like that.'

I asked who were the officers of this philanthropic body.

'Oh, myself, and the Colonel, and Sammy and Lord Orris and Sir Gerald and Joe and Briggs and one or two more—'

I smiled.

'So Brensham still hangs together,' I said. 'How much does it cost to become a Vice-President?'

When I had paid my half-guinea Mr Chorlton said:

'Seriously, the village is pretty hard up; and I'm worried about it for a particular reason. Lately there's been a long-nosed, evil-looking, squint-eyed snooping lawyer driving about the place in a large and expensive car. He seems to be on the look-out for any little property that might, in consequence of our poverty, come into the market cheap.'

'He came to see me,' said Alfie. 'Bloke in a bowler hat and black coat and pin-striped trousers—'

'That's the one. Did he offer to buy your land?'

'He said he thought he could put me in touch with a purchaser.'

'That's the johnny. What did you say?'

'I said I didn't want to sell. I'd rather wait till the bank sells me up.' Alfie grinned. 'Who is he?'

'I don't know,' said Mr Chorlton, 'but I have a brother who's a stockbroker in London, and therefore has to meet some rather shady people from time to time. He was lunching, the other day, with some of these customers and they were talking about Brensham. So he perked up and listened knowing I lived here.'

'What did they say?' I asked.

'Not much, but it struck me as a little sinister. They said,' concluded Mr Chorlton '– in the hateful and blood-curdling language of their kind – they said they thought we were Ripe for Development, that's all.'

PART FIVE

THE GROUPERS

*Death of the Rector – The Old Schoolmaster – The Groupers
Arrive – The Garden-party – The Converts – No more Cakes
and Ale – The Meeting – And Ginger Shall Be Hot i' the
Mouth too – C. of E. – End of an Episode*

Death of the Rector

FOR A LONG while Mr Mountjoy had been growing
more frail, more forgetful, and more haphazard in the
performance of his parish duties. I believe there was no
truth in the story that, having stored some live bait in his
font in anticipation of a day's pike-fishing, he forgot to
remove them before the next christening; so that the infant
was sprinkled with minnows and baptized with bleak. But it
was certainly true that he took snuff in his pulpit, pausing in
the middle of his sermon to help himself from a silver snuff-
box with a small silver spoon. And I know that he went
fishing, not only in his biretta, but in his cassock as well; for
the last time I saw him he was worming for perch, in this
rather unsuitable dress, from the landing-stage below
Sammy Hunt's cottage. He had found a shoal of these
confiding fishes, and was happily engaged in pulling them
out one after another.

'Truly,' he said to me, 'old Izaak Walton accurately

described them when he said they were like the wicked of this world, not afraid, though their friends and companions perish in their sight!'

It was a paradox that the more eccentric the Rector became and the more outrageous his behaviour grew, the better the village liked him; so that at the end even his churchwardens, who had frequently complained to the Bishop about his scandalous conduct, were heard to declare that for all his faults he was the best parson the parish had ever had. He died, from a failing heart, in late November. He had never, in all his long cure, made any special effort to persuade his parishioners to go to church, and for thirty years he had preached, rather badly, to half-empty pews. He might have smiled, therefore, if he could have seen the crowd at his funeral, which overflowed into the churchyard because there was not enough room for it. But he was one of the gentlest Christians I ever knew; and there would have been no bitterness in his smile.

He was succeeded by a man called Wilkinson who immediately astonished the villagers by smiting them powerfully upon their backs and shoulders and addressing them by such terms of affection as 'Dear boy', 'Old fellow' and even 'Gaffer'. In his conversation, and sometimes in his sermons, he frequently used such expressions as 'scrumptious', 'ripping', and 'awfully jolly'. He spoke with a slight lisp, and his Christian name was Cecil. When I asked Mr Chorlton what he thought of him, he hesitated before answering and eventually said:

'What can one think about an overgrown Boy Scout who obviously means well? I suggest, however, that William Wordsworth described him beautifully in the worst line ever written by a great poet.'

'And what is the line?' I asked.

'"A Mr Wilkinson, a clergyman." Simply that.'

The Old Schoolmaster

'But of course,' remarked Mr Chorlton later on. 'You mustn't take much notice of what I say; for I am getting to an age when a man has an abhorrence of new régimes and when every trifling change seems to be a reminder of mortality. I cling to my old books, my old port and my old friends as if they were rocks amid the shifting sands of the world. The example of History tells me that there will be books written as wise as Plato's, Burgundy produced as good as the Romanée-Conti of which I once possessed a dozen, and claret as good as Chateau Lafite 1870; and that new friends might prove as true as old ones. And I answer, This is certainly so, but I am sixty-six next birthday, and my eyes get tired with reading, my digestion is worn out with experimenting, and my temper is quickly exhausted by fools. I have no time to go whoring after new things.'

Mr Chorlton was in a mood of deep depression, which was very rare with him. He had recently retired from his job as Assistant Master at the preparatory school near Elmbury where he had taught the Classics for nearly forty years. He hated giving it up; but the old Head Master, who had been as a brother to him, had died, and the school had been sold to a young man, who, as young men will, at once began to make radical changes. 'I knew he was a mathematician as soon as I looked at him,' said Mr Chorlton, 'and I knew that he would have no respect for tradition in consequence.' He substituted rugger for soccer in the Easter term and the English Hymnal for Hymns A and M in chapel. He revised the old-fashioned syllabus and introduced new subjects such as Physiology and Modelling. ('As if,' said Mr Chorlton, 'a country boy were incapable of discovering for himself about the sex-life of butterflies and as if he had to be *taught* to play

with plasticine!') However, these reforms did not seriously
affect Mr Chorlton himself and he carried on contentedly
enough with his teaching of the Classics until one day the
Head Master decided that the school must adopt the New
Pronunciation of Latin.

'This was too much,' he told me afterwards. 'I had no
choice but to resign.' And indeed it was impossible to con-
ceive that Mr Chorlton, who had begun the spring term
every year for forty years with *Arma virumque cano* . . . should
adapt himself to saying *Weerumque*.

'I should have had to pronounce the accusative plural of
causa,' he said, 'as if I were referring to the behind of a cow.
I should have had to tell my boys that Julius Caesar, a hook-
nosed tough, reported his conquest of England in a sort of
sissy's squeak of *Wayny, weedy, weeky*! No: I am too old for
such nonsense. I had to go.'

But now that the holidays were over and yet he remained
on holiday, he was restless and lonely and the years of his
retirement, which he had often looked forward to, stretched
in front of him empty and grey. Certainly he had plenty of
hobbies to amuse him: his entomology, reading, cricket,
wine; but there remained a gap in his life unfilled and he
missed, I think, the things which old schoolmasters so
absurdly miss, the scamper of feet in the corridor, the chatter
of young voices, the rows of dull or lively faces which never
change nor grow old although the piece of Unseen through
which Williams Major blindly fumbles his way is the same
passage which his father, then Williams Minor, clumsily
stumbled through in the same form-room twenty-five years
ago.

The Groupers Arrive

Brensham had put up with the Rector's back-slappings, shoulder-thumpings, and schoolboyish endearments for about three months when he held his first 'house-party' and let loose upon the astonished village some two-score members of the Oxford Group.

There wasn't room for them all at the Rectory, so the overflows were boarded out at the Horse Narrow, the Trumpet, and the Adam and Eve. The landlords of all three had had a bad winter, and they were very glad to make a few pounds by letting their rooms so early in the season. 'Whatever you says about the Parson,' said Joe Trentfield, 'he's the first parson I've ever heard of who was good for trade.' However, I don't think even Joe bargained for the remarkable assortment of visitors who arrived at the Horse Narrow on Friday evening. He didn't know much about the Oxford Group, but he had vaguely expected some sort of grave ecclesiastical conclave: if not of clergymen, at any rate lay brothers or foreign missioners or the kind of prim elderly ladies who organize Scripture readings or arrange for copies of the Bible to be placed in the bedrooms of commercial hotels. He was somewhat taken aback, therefore, when he discovered that his quota of guests included two bouncing gym-mistresses, a Lett who spoke little English and a Lithuanian who spoke none, and a middle-aged American lady who talked about Gard with ease and assurance but rather in the way she would speak of a President of the United States.

After closing-time Joe took a walk up the village street and called on Jim Hartley at the Adam and Eve.

'What kind of queer fish has the Rector sent *you*?' he inquired.

'Rum 'uns,' said Jim. 'They may be very religious but they're certainly rum. I've got a Frog and a couple of Huns, and a pretty little piece who looks like an actress, and one of those huntin' shootin' women, and – Joe—'

'Yes, Jim?'

'I've got a bloke with his head close-cropped who always talks out of the corner of his mouth. What'd you say about him?'

'I'd say he'd probably just come out of jug.'

'And I should say,' said Jim with awe, 'that it won't be very long before he goes back there!'

Next day, as it happened, we played the first cricket-match of the season; and after the match we went to the Adam and Eve for our usual game of darts. The bar, however, was so full of the Rector's guests that there was no room for us, and we went on to the Horse Narrow. Joe's bar was crowded too, but we decided to make the best of a bad job and stay there. Before we knew what was happening we found ourselves involved in conversation with a number of hearty young men and women who told us that their Christian names were Alan, Mabel, Betty, Ernest, Sigrid and Harry, and asked us to tell them ours.

Within a few moments Mr Chorlton had been captured by an attractive-looking if slightly hysterical girl who discoursed to him on the subject of Absolute Truth; another girl was talking earnestly to Alfie upon some matter which seemed to cause him the profoundest embarrassment; Sir Gerald listened courteously to a blond youth who told him gravely: 'I assure you, sir, even my lawn-tennis has improved since I brought religion into it.' As for me, I was cornered by the Lett whose English appeared to be limited to a single and ambiguous phrase. 'Yes, by damn, no!' he shouted enthusiastically, in answer to every question; 'No, by damn, yes?' he would interrogate me by way of variation if for a few moments through sheer exhaustion I fell silent.

There was such a great deal of chatter, so much high shrill laughter, so many boisterous cries of 'Old Boy' and 'Dear Fellow' that you could hardly hear Mimi's strumming upon the piano at the other end of the room. When Joe passed me a beer across the counter he whispered:

'I likes to see 'em enjoying 'emselves, but 'tis a wonder to me how they does it, on ginger-pop.'

I now perceived that none of the Groupers drank beer, but consumed numerous fizzy drinks such as lemonade, Cydrax, or raspberry squash.

'Tell me,' I said to the Lett, 'are you all teetotallers?'

He clicked his heels and bowed.

'Yes, by damn, no!' he yelled.

Over his shoulder the blond tennis-player spoke up to inform me:

'It's not a matter of principle, old fellow; nothing priggish or Blue Ribbon about it; but if God tells you, in your QT, to give it up, well, you give it up, that's all. He told me to stop smoking, too.'

'QT?' I asked, bewildered. 'What's QT?'

'Quiet Times, old man. After breakfast.'

'It's like being on the transatlantic telephone,' said the American lady, 'but you never get a wrong number from Gard.'

I glanced at Billy Butcher, who was standing next to her and he gave me a slow wink. He was in one of his clowning moods and I watched him put on his rather vacuous Andrew-Aguecheek look before he announced innocently:

'Really, I ought to try it. I'm the most frightful hopeless drunkard that ever was.'

They gathered round him at once like wasps round a pot of honey.

'No, honestly, you aren't *really*?' said the attractive girl who had been talking to Mr Chorlton.

'Honestly, I'm afraid, incurable,' said Billy. 'No medicine in the world can do me good.' (I thought: by God, that's true, and I wonder if he really knows it.)

'But *our* medicine,' said the American lady, her eyes shining, 'is not of this world at all, it comes from Gard.'

I edged away, and left Billy to his fooling. It was his own business, I thought, if he liked to pull their legs; but I found it, somehow, a trifle embarrassing and I was glad of the opportunity to slip away into a corner and talk to David Groves about the plague of rabbits in the railway-cutting. The Groupers, no doubt, were just silly and adolescent and probably harmless; but they were alien to Brensham and to the Horse Narrow and our pub wasn't the same, our cricket-evening was utterly spoiled, because of their presence. Almost everybody, except the Groupers, looked a bit uncomfortable and constrained; and only Sammy was entirely happy, for he had got hold of the Lithuanian who couldn't speak English and was telling him, without the least risk of interruption, the story of the geisha girl at Yokohama.

The Garden-party

On Sunday afternoon the Rector and his wife gave a garden-party on the Rectory lawn to which the whole village was bidden. Mr Chorlton and I went butterfly-hunting instead, and spent a pleasant day on the hill; we had an account of the party later from Billy Butcher, who attended it. The tea, we learned, had been followed by a meeting, at which the Groupers made speeches and talked very informally about God and about their sins. The girl who had been an actress spoke on the subject of Absolute Purity and the man who looked like a convict on Absolute Honesty; a young woman called Mabel described Absolute Truth. ('Yes,' said Mr Chorlton, 'I listened to her last night. She is un-educated, empty-headed and shallow; but, bless her heart, she believes she has discovered what all the philosophers from Socrates downwards have searched for in vain!') Then the blond young man had electrified the meeting by declaring: 'If you ask me who is the best tennis coach in the world I shall answer quite simply: God.' He was followed by a Bright Young Thing who warned her audience that her speech would be a teeny-weeny bit shame-making. It was.

'And then,' said Billy, 'I said a few words—'

'Billy!' exclaimed Mr Chorlton. 'Don't you think you're playing a rather silly game?'

'It gave them pleasure,' said Billy, 'and I enjoyed it. I can't see that it did any harm.'

'What did you tell them?' I asked.

'I described to them in great detail the sensations of a man suffering from the willies.'

Mr Chorlton said gravely:

'Have you ever had them, Billy?'

A cloud passed briefly over Billy's face.

'Twice,' he said. 'Once in West Africa and once in the ship coming home. They're hell.'

I changed the subject. 'Who was at the party besides yourself?' I said. 'From the village, I mean.'

'Sammy. Briggs. The Trentfields. Mrs Hartley and Jim. Sir Gerald and his wife. Lord Orris and Jane. Alfie. Mrs Doan and Sally and a few more.'

'Any converts?' I said.

Billy looked curiously embarrassed. 'Well,' he said, 'I – er – don't know exactly. I suppose there might have been one or two.'

The Converts

It seems astonishing, in retrospect, that this transatlantic hysteria should have had any effect upon Brensham at all other than to shock it, for Brensham is old and wise, its roots go deep into English history, and its religious tradition is tolerant, easy-going, and unfervent. Revivalists of various persuasions have passed through our countryside at various times, and provoked no more response than a shrug of the shoulders or a raised eyebrow for all their hymn-singing and their oratory. However, the Rector and his Oxford Groupers did succeed in making a few converts at first and they certainly 'changed' one or two lives, though they may not necessarily have changed them for the better.

The first of these converts were Mrs Doan and Sally; and they were converted, not by the Groupers, but by Billy. His foolish leg-pull, begun with a jest and carried on in a mood of savage clowning, had a consequence which he certainly had not anticipated. Mrs Doan, silly but kind, who had mothered him for years as if he had been her own wayward son, naturally concluded that there must be something good in any religion or revival which held out the prospect of curing him of drinking. As for Sally, she was young, she was infatuated, and she was feather-brained; she longed, as all young people do, for a Cause, and here was a Cause which she could identify with Love. After Billy's speech, Sally had rushed up to him and cried:

'Oh Billy, I'm – so – so pleased.'

'So . . . so happy about it, Billy dear,' echoed her mother. And, to make his shame and embarrassment all the greater, they had kissed him, while the triumphant Groupers, moved beyond measure, could scarcely forbear to cheer.

Subsequent conversions were less emotional and, perhaps,

somewhat less complete. Sir Gerald Hope-Kingley, for instance, who rather hesitantly and for a very short time dabbled about on the fringe of the Group without becoming very deeply involved in it, did so because he was a Potterer – his Alpines had failed again – and no opportunity for Pottering came amiss to him. (In the same spirit he had dabbled in Buddhism, Christian Science, and Spiritualism, and at one time, he told us, had practically made up his mind to become a Moslem.) Jeremy Briggs also joined the Group, because he thought, at first, that it was Democratic; and also because it gave him the opportunity to make political speeches thinly disguised as affirmations of religious faith. And Mrs Hartley joined it for the simple reason that she was a bit of a snob and it delighted her to address the gentry, even if most of them were foreign gentry, by their Christian names.

But other of the villagers, for various reasons, disliked the activities of the Rector and his friends, and were shocked, embarrassed, or merely amused by them. Joe Trentfield, who held the soldierly view that Niggers began at Calais, disapproved of the presence in Brensham of so many foreigners. 'Mark my words,' he said, 'there's something behind it' – and when we asked him what was behind it he whispered darkly: 'Religion has been used as cover for spying before now.' Alfie Perks, who had only been to church about three times in his life, was scandalized by the Groupers' public confession of their sins, and declared firmly: 'There's only one religion for me, and that's Church of England.' Lord Orris, too gentle and too courteous to blame or criticize, nevertheless when asked his opinion would sigh and shake his head. Jane, who declared herself an atheist but secretly, I think, longed for a Faith she could fight and die for, failed to find one in the Oxford Group; she thought its members were 'soft, stupid and vulgar'. Old

David Groves, being asked by the Rector to call him by his Christian name, was so upset that he fled from the meeting. The Colonel who had been a regular churchgoer in the old Rector's day, was so profoundly shocked by the whole business that he exclaimed fiercely: 'I shall never enter the church again' – and then, with one of his sudden smiles, added an amendment: 'Until they carry me there!'

No more Cakes and Ale

Throughout the summer the Groupers came and went, mainly at weekends, and for the most part Brensham shrugged its shoulders and regarded them as a small recurrent nuisance like the buzzing of flies. Mrs Hartley, however, continued to make Jim's life a misery because she had received Guidance to the effect that he was getting too fat, and had obediently cut down his meals to two a day, while denying him the customary snacks and trifles such as chitterlings and sardines on toast with which she had stayed his pangs of hunger at mid-morning. For breakfast she allowed him two small pieces of Ryvita without any butter.

The Group lost one adherent, for Sir Gerald bought a book on the Pyramids which persuaded him that there was a great deal of truth in the teaching of the British Israelites; and they gained one, for Sammy Hunt suddenly and quite unaccountably joined them. This distressed us, for we were very fond of Sammy in spite of the fact that his tales grew longer and his determination to tell them became more unshakable as time went by. But as Joe Trentfield said wisely: 'Sailors are great ones for queer religions. 'Tis the loneliness in the ships as sets 'em thinking; and they catches funny ideas from folks like the heathen Chinee. Once a sailor always a sailor; so Sammy's susceptible to religion as some people are to colds. He'll get over it soon.' And indeed, Sammy didn't seem at all happy in his new faith. In contrast to the scrubbed and smiling faces of the Groupers his was as long as a wet week; and when he encountered us he gave us a small sideways look and hurried on, like a dog that has been naughty.

Mr Wilkinson, meanwhile, continued to rush about the village patting people on the back; and when you addressed him as 'Rector' he would invite you, with a toothy smile: 'Call me Thistle.' Brensham accepted his invitation and called him Thistle henceforth; but not to his face.

The Groupers, of course, would have addressed the Holy Apostles themselves by their Christian names; or rather they would have abbreviated them and called Saint Peter Pete. So you heard Sally Doan saying of the Rector: 'I think Cecil's so wonderful' and you learned for the first time the unexpected Christian name of Sally's mother: which was Dolores.

These two, I think, enjoyed themselves more than anybody else in Brensham during that strange uncomfortable summer; for all women delight in reforming the men they love, and they were completely convinced that Billy, if not already cured, was well on the way towards reformation. It would be untrue to say that the Group had 'changed' Billy; nothing could do that; but with the aid of the Doans it had nearly succeeded in breaking him. He crept about wretchedly, frightened of his old friends and terrified of the Doans, loathing the attentive Groupers, loathing himself, and yet perhaps half attracted as well as half repelled by the promise of hearts-ease which the new faith seemed to offer him.

'We're so *proud* of you, Billy,' the Groupers would tell him several times a day; and indeed they were, for their attitude towards him was that of anglers towards an enormous fish which they have just landed. And Sally Doan would look at him with wide bright ecstatic eyes and tell him: 'Yes, Billy, we're all so proud.'

Why had he ever risen to their bait, so obligingly hooked himself, swum with hardly a kick or a wriggle into their landing-net? I don't know; but I think Billy of late had become increasingly aware that he had reached the end of his tether. I had seen him, sometimes, in the mornings before he had his first drink and I had wondered how he managed even to drag himself down to the Adam and Eve. Once I had watched him, when he failed after three attempts to lift his glass, tie a handkerchief to his wrist, pass it round the back of his neck, and use the arrangement as a pulley by which he raised the drink to his lips. He couldn't go on much longer like that; and when the Groupers' tinselly bait swam into his ken he played with it at first as a savage jest and then seized it as a sort of suicide. It was that or DTs.

Now he had given up drinking; the Groupers, Mrs Doan and Sally saw to that between them, for they hardly left him alone for a moment during the day. They 'entertained' him; they took him for picnics on the hill; they even brought him into the pub and bought him peppermint cordial and ginger wine. But they never left him alone there; for they were not going to let the biggest fish they'd ever hooked flop back down the slippery slope into the river.

As far as possible, we kept out of his way, for he appeared embarrassed in our company and we felt it only fair to give the Groupers a chance to 'change' him or 'save' him or whatever it was they were trying to do. But I met him once in the Horse Narrow, with the blond tennis-player who held that God was a good sport and the young man from Latvia who doled him out his ginger wine and who had apparently been detailed as his keeper or guard. Billy raised his glass to me and said: 'Down the hatch, boys' with a rather pathetic imitation of his old manner; and then he whispered to me over his shoulder: 'They're trying to do a Watts-Dunton on me, old chap.' 'Yes, by damn, no!' said the Lett loudly, clicking his heels.

The Meeting

In August the Rector took the Village Hall for another meeting. It was fruit-picking time, and Brensham's busiest season; so the village had a good excuse to stay away. However, there was quite a large audience, for we had heard that Pistol, Bardolph and Nym would be present to testify to the change in their lives; and that was something we would not miss if we could help it. Tidings had reached Elmbury of the strange happenings at Brensham; and the three musketeers had decided to find out whether there was any profit to be made out of them. It seemed there was; for they arrived on a motor-bike and sidecar, and all three were wearing new suits. The Rector made a short speech in which he said that the Oxford Group, although its aim was spiritual, had recently demonstrated that it could do practical good as well. Those three old soldiers, whose lives had been so wonderfully changed, had pointed out that their infirmities and the effect of past wounds prevented them from getting about the country to attend the numerous meetings which were now being organized by the Group; therefore a few of the Groupers, who wished to remain anonymous, had subscribed between them enough money to buy the motor-cycle combination which tonight had been ridden for the first time . . .

This speech was received with loud cheers; for there were a large number of Fitchers and Gormleys at the back of the hall, who had heard with wonder and unbelief of the conversion of Pistol, Bardolph and Nym and had immediately concluded that the Group must provide a happy hunting-ground for scroungers. They were gratified to find that they had been right; and they stared with envy at the smart new suits of Pistol, Bardolph and Nym who sat with great assurance upon the platform.

The American lady spoke, and a gentleman from Helsinki said a few words, and then Billy Butcher made a very strange and confused speech which caused many of his hearers to suspect that he had been drinking again although his keepers gave the assurance that he had had nothing but ginger wine; for his face was flushed and his words were mainly inaudible, and he finished up by quoting, irrelevantly, the Groupers thought, a long extract from Swinburne's Hymn to Proserpine. At the end of this recitation he shouted in a loud voice *Vicisti, Galileae*, and sat down.

However, the speeches of Pistol, Bardolph and Nym made up for Billy's unfortunate lapse. Pistol affirmed that he had been in prison eighteen times; Bardolph overbid him with twenty; and Nym, outdoing them both, declared that he had been incarcerated not only twenty-five times but in six different countries. The Fitchers and Gormleys cheered, the Groupers clapped, and 'Bravo, bravo!' cried the Rector.

'I ain't proud of it, mind,' whined Nym. 'I 'angs me 'ead in shame.'

'Aye,' said Pistol.

'Ar,' said Bardolph.

And Billy, forgetting for the moment his own misery, looked at them across the platform and winked.

The speeches over, the Rector got up to make his final appeal; but there was a great deal of noise going on at the back of the hall and he found difficulty in making himself heard. 'Silence for the Rector!' cried Pistol in a loud voice. 'Let Mr Wilkinson have his say!' echoed Nym. The Rector allowed his hands to rest upon their shoulders while he waited for the noise to subside. 'Call me Thistle, dear boys,' he whispered. 'Call me Thistle.'

But alas, the disturbing noise grew louder. It had begun as a low menacing mutter; and indeed the Groupers had taken it for applause. Now it swelled in volume and took the shape of a rhythmic chanting, like that of primitive tribes, and amid the increasing pandemonium the amazed occupants of the platform were able at last to distinguish the words:

'What's in the salmon-nets today-ay?
What's in the salmon-nets today?'

The Groupers, knowing nothing of village history and believing that the chanted meaningless question was directed at themselves, quailed and sought escape; the tennis-player with great presence of mind slipped out through a side-door and ran to fetch the policeman. Shouts and dreadful oaths now interrupted the chant; there was a yell of pain followed by a scuffling of feet, there were cries of 'Wife stealers!' 'Gallows birds!' and 'Murderers' and suddenly pandemonium reigned, as the doors at the rear of the hall burst open and a score of screaming, pummelling, kicking Gormleys followed by a score of screeching, biting, scratching Fitchers rushed forth and passed in headlong rout down the peaceful village street of Brensham.

And Ginger Shall Be Hot i' the Mouth too

The Colonel was a man who knew a great deal about drink and drinking; I do not mean that he was in the precise sense of the word a connoisseur, but he was at least able to deliver a sound judgement upon the alcoholic content of any liquid you put in front of him. Therefore we were both surprised and interested when he said to Joe Trentfield one night in the Horse Narrow:

'Give me a double ginger wine, Joe. I believe the beastly stuff has a kick in it.'

While Joe brought his drink the Colonel nodded in the direction of Billy Butcher, who was standing at the other end of the bar with the Lett, the tennis-player, and Sally Doan.

'It is just possible,' he said, 'that the ginger wine in some curious way has become fermented. There is no other explanation. For if you can tell me of any non-alcoholic drink which will make a man's eyes as red as a ferret's, cause him to stagger whenever he lets go of the bar, and provoke him to quote poetry, I'll eat my hat. And on account of the fish-hooks in it that might prove indigestible.'

The Lett, who had learned a little English, came across to the Colonel and said:

'I see you also by damn on water-wagon! Dam' good! Billie he stick to non-alk three weeks. Dam' good. Life changed. God does it. Maybe He do you too, dam' miracle, yes by damn no!'

The Colonel lifted his drink, smelt it, sipped it and rolled it round his tongue. A look of acute distaste passed over his features. 'I thought so,' he said. 'By God, I thought so! The President of the Blue Ribbon League couldn't get drunk on a gallon.' The expression of distaste faded; and suddenly his rough winter face softened into spring. A zephyr crossed it, then another, and he smiled as the orchards smile in blossom-time; but behind the zephyr came the breeze, and soon the Colonel began to laugh, and the breeze freshened into a strong wind and the wind into a gale; a huge hurri-cane of laughter shook him as he leaned across the bar to

Joe and whispered: 'Now then, you rogue, the secret's out. What do you put in it? Gin?'

Joe nodded.

'He came to me and said he couldn't stand it any longer; would I slip a double gin into it every time he asked for a glass of ginger wine? Well, Colonel, how could I refuse? He looked that miserable, and you know I likes to see people enjoying themselves. 'Twas common charity to do it; and he squares up prompt and regular at the end of the week. Besides 'twas my opinion the teetotal stuff was killing him quicker nor the spirits would.'

'Ah well,' said the Colonel, 'it's a nice point of morals; and I'm blowed if I know whether the Recording Angel will put it to the debit or credit of your account. Meanwhile for God's sake take the nasty stuff away and give me a large whisky!'

At the other end of the bar, to the applauding Lett, the puzzled tennis-player, and the utterly uncomprehending Sally, Billy was quoting at great length from *Hamlet*.

C. of E.

'*Stulta Maritali jam porrigit ora capistro*,' said Mr Chorlton with a sigh. 'At last he stretches out his foolish head to the conjugal halter.' We had just come from the wedding of Billy Butcher to Sally Doan, Spinster of Brensham parish, and now Mr Chorlton and I walked back through the churchyard while the Groupers continued to entertain bride and bridegroom at an uproarious party on the Rectory lawn. After all, it was their little triumph; for good or ill it was the only positive thing they had achieved at Brensham. The rest of their few converts were already beginning to melt away. Sammy Hunt had left them, and now when he met us he looked more than ever like a dog who is conscious that it has made a mess in the corner. Jeremy Briggs had discovered that Democracy is not simply achieved through calling everybody by their Christian names, and finding what he described as 'the seeds of Fascism' among some of the Groupers he had angrily walked out of one of their meetings, swearing he would never return. Even Mrs Hartley was beginning to doubt the validity of her after-breakfast Guidance as Jim became more morose and ill-tempered every day. Only Sally Doan, her mother and Billy remained; and with these last pieces upon the chess-board the Groupers played out their disastrous game. They were well-meaning, of course; they were quite sure, terrifyingly sure, that they were God's instruments in doing good; and what more obvious example of doing good than to complete the supposed reformation of Billy Butcher by providing him with a devoted wife, and a mother-in-law who was almost as possessive as a mother, to look after him till death them did part?

'What a Human Story!' whispered the Rector to Mr Chorlton in the church porch. 'And what a Happy Ending!'

It had been, however, an uncomfortable ceremony. Billy, in a mood of savage acquiescence, had obviously taken a good many 'ginger wines' beforehand to sustain himself; he came to his wedding with the swaggering devil-may-care of Petruchio but without Petruchio's gaiety, and both within the church and at the reception indulged in so much clumsy clowning that even foolish doting Mrs Doan looked alarmed and fluttered in agitation like an old hen. But Sally seemed ecstatically happy; her bright eyes shone and she wore the expression of one who is about to undergo a willing and a joyful martyrdom. It was clear that she had Dedicated her Life to the redemption of Billy. But Mr

Chorlton looked at the matter in a different light. 'She has been Butchered,' he said, 'to make a Grouper's holiday.'

Now he paused at the lych-gate to light his pipe, and looked back at the airy spire of our lovely church, and said:

'You know, John, it is a very curious thing. I am an agnostic, and I find in all religions, including the Christian one, a perpetual affront to my reason: and yet I find too, deep in my heart, a real and growing affection for this Church of England. Why?'

He paused and puffed hard to get his pipe going.

'Now why?' he went on. 'Historically it is absurd, being the bastard child of a king's folly and a pope's obstinacy; born of accident and compromise, with a breath of puritanical brimstone at its christening which doesn't seem to have done it any harm. Its dogma is so confused that even its Bishops have difficulty in defining it, and end up by allowing their flock to believe anything, everything or nothing so long as they refrain from causing a scandal. The structure of its doctrine is as much a mixture of different styles and periods as the physical structure of our church, which is a blend of early Norman, late Norman, fourteenth century and Perp, with a three-decker pulpit and an octagonal font in which old Mountjoy, rest his soul, used to keep his little fishes. And a lot of perfectly odious late-Victorian windows presented by Lord Orris' father! But the building is homogeneous, isn't it – almost as much part of the landscape as the hedges and the trees? Now look at its doctrine; take a slice of the Reformation, spice it with English puritanism and butter it with English tolerance, add a pinch of popery, boil it in English Conservatism, and garnish it with all the extraordinary odds and ends such as Establishment and Tithe, Queen Anne's Bounty and the Parson's Glebe and the Ecclesiastical Commissioners. What a recipe! And then bear in mind the fact that a country living may be in the gift of a layman who doesn't believe in Christianity at all or a squire whose only anxiety is to appoint a clergyman who hunts and plays a good game of bridge! And yet,' repeated Mr Chorlton, leaning on the wall beside the wicket-gate, 'I love it. Agnostic though I am, I want to be buried in this churchyard when I die, and I should be very content for some absurd old clergyman such as Mountjoy to say over me those splendid words in the Burial Service: dust to dust and ashes to ashes. The funny thing is that thousands of people who don't believe in it have the same feeling. I suppose in Greece and Rome, when the old Gods fell out of favour and people ceased to believe in their thunderbolts and their power, the crumbling ivy-grown altars were still regarded with a sort of half-amused, half-apologetic affection, and people made an occasional shame-faced sacrifice at them for old time's sake. That is how I feel about the C. of E. and I still wonder why!'

It was a perfect September afternoon, and the spire rose steeply above us into a blue sky. The swifts swept round it, screeching as they hunted flies. A thrush was cracking snails against the gravestones in the churchyard, and I noticed that Mr Mountjoy's nesting-boxes hadn't yet been removed from the church porch. Mr Chorlton went on:

'I suppose the answer is that it's not a system but a spirit: as Gilbert Murray said of Plato. It has grown up with England, and its history is largely hers. It has suckled on her wisdom and fed on her tolerance. It isn't, thank goodness, militant here on earth, and it doesn't want to torture or burn or excommunicate people who disagree with it. It just keeps its doors open for anybody who wants to come in. And inside there's no ranting nonsense nor anything to shock us or embarrass us or make us think too deeply. A healing draught if you like that sort of thing, but no strong poison. I once had a friend who was the most easy-going chap I ever knew; and he summed up his whole doctrine in a single sentence: "*It doesn't matter what you do so long as you don't frighten the horses.*" Surely that's our attitude in this part of England; we've never been troubled by Irish Shouters, Welsh Jumpers, Cornish Revivalists or any sort of dancing dervishes before; and we don't like 'em.'

He glanced across towards the Rectory garden, where the Groupers were playing some absurd game which looked rather like leapfrog. He made a dismissive gesture with his hand.

'That midsummer madness will pass,' he said. 'It is brief and evanescent. It has no roots. It isn't part of the pattern. Indeed I think, as far as Brensham is concerned, it is passing already. It commits the unforgivable sin: it frightens the horses.'

End of an Episode

And indeed, before the leaves fell, the strange episode was over. The Rector and his proselytizing young wife lost heart and hope suddenly. For six months they had laid siege to our citadel with no more success than the taking of a few hostages and the temporary breach, perhaps, of a bastion or an outer wall. But Brensham quickly repaired the breach, and the hostages began to come back to us one by one: Sammy, Briggs and at last Mrs Hartley, who devoted her days to the concoction of tasty dishes and the preparation of innumerable snacks for Jim, to make up for his months of privation. Then Pistol, Bardolph and Nym, having decided that there was no more to be got out of the Groupers, sold their motor-bike and sidecar for forty pounds and began to drink the proceeds; but this process was interrupted when Bardolph, becoming incapable, and Nym, becoming disorderly, were both sent to prison. Pistol soberly awaited their release; for he had no pleasure in drinking alone.

Soon the Rector's 'house-parties' became smaller. ('A good thing,' said Joe Trentfield, 'for really, we never felt our daughters were really safe, with all those Niggers about.') At last they ceased altogether in consequence of a most unfortunate happening which occurred in early October. There had been, for several weeks, a minor epidemic of burglary and petty larceny in the district: Sir Gerald's house had been broken into and so had Lord Orris' (though the luckless thief found nothing worth stealing there). Then, one night, Banks intercepted the man who looked like a convict walking towards Elmbury with a heavy suitcase in his hand. This proved to be full of an assortment of articles which the Rector later identified as his silver spoons, fish-knives, gold watch, Venetian glasses, and his wife's diamond ring. In court the culprit asked for eleven other offences to be taken into consideration. When asked if he had anything to say, he pleaded humorously: 'The temptation, your Honour, was put in my way. It was too much for an old lag. They were so simple!'

'A fair enough comment,' said Mr Chorlton when he read the report in the local paper. 'It would serve as a not-unkindly epitaph: *They were so simple!*'

There were no house-parties after that. Shortly the Rector was offered another living, perhaps in some parish where the villagers were less mistrustful of strange and new things. He readily accepted, and his successor turned out to be a kindly old man whose hobby was numismatics and whose only ambition was the enjoyment of peace and quiet so that he might finish before he died his book of seven hundred pages on the *Theology of St Thomas Aquinas*.

PART SIX

THE SYNDICATE

'To the Workhouse with Him' – Ruin and Rabbits – . . . Musa vetat mori – The Postman – The Oppressors – The Last Crusade – The Vultures Descend – The Mad Lord Discovers Dreamland – Many a True Word – The Right of Way – The New Unhappy Lords – The Secret People – This Desirable Property – ' . . . of Interest to Speculators and Others'

'To the Workhouse with Him'

THE HUGE and horrid Syndicate, meanwhile, consolidated its position upon the slopes and the summit of Brensham Hill; and Lord Orris continued to keep himself out of the Bankruptcy Court by selling, to the Syndicate, a covert, a few fields or a small parcel of land every time they threatened to foreclose on the mortgage. Thus his estate suffered a gradual attrition, and now only his Park, the Manor, the Home Orchard and a few adjoining small-holdings and cottages remained to him and were like an island amid the encroaching flood. Lately he had been compelled to sacrifice the Folly, which his great-great-grandfather had built in 1755. It stood in a rough field overgrown with brambles and thorn-bushes, which the Syndicate had long coveted because their pheasants, bred in the larch plantation, were apt to stray there. They had no use for the Folly itself, and they certainly had none for the Hermit who inevitably went with it. They lost no time in applying for an ejectment order against him, and their lawyer took pains to emphasize that in doing so they displayed remarkable tolerance and clemency. 'My clients,' he said, 'cannot recognize him as any sort of a tenant, not even a tenant-at-will; indeed it is possible that in the eyes of the law he is simply a tresspasser. I am instructed that he more or less "lives off the land" and if this is so he could also be prosecuted for tresspassing in pursuit of coneys. But in view of the fact that he appears to have committed this trespass with Lord Orris' consent or acquiescence for a great number of years I have advised my clients to take the very moderate course of applying for this order.'

I am sure that Lord Orris, when he made over the field on which the Folly stood, had no idea that he was throwing the Hermit to the wolves; it simply had not occurred to him that anybody would want to turn the poor old man out. General Bouverie and the rest of the magistrates apparently felt the same; it was obvious that they were unhappy about the case, for the General asked:

'Do your clients offer him any alternative accommodation?'

'Emphatically no, your Worship. They do not regard him as a suitable tenant for any of their cottages, even if one were vacant.'

The magistrates consulted together. At last General Bouverie said:

'The man is very old: and although he is certainly a little eccentric the Bench feels that it would be somewhat harsh to turn him out, at his age, with nowhere to go except the workhouse, of which he would probably be a rather difficult inmate.'

'I must repeat,' said the long-nosed lawyer, 'that for

various sanitary reasons which I need not go into, my clients regard him as a most undesirable tenant: if indeed he can be called a tenant. They are being very lenient, but I am afraid they feel strongly on the subject; for the Tower, in its present condition, is nothing short of a menace to public health.'

The General said drily:

'Really? On the top of Brensham Hill?'

'Certainly,' snapped the lawyer. 'The water supply of several villages is dependent upon springs which are found within a few hundred yards of the Tower.'

He sat down. The magistrates consulted again, and then General Bouverie announced brusquely: 'Application granted. The order will be made.' He had no choice, for the case was clear-cut and simple, and he knew that even if he adjourned it the Syndicate would marshal against the wretched Hermit all the formidable bureaucratic apparatus of Sanitary Inspectors, Medical Officers of Health and perhaps the Lunacy Laws.

However, it proved less simple to get rid of the Hermit than it was to issue the order; for he sat down upon his dirty pile of straw and flatly refused to budge. When a second attempt was made he shut himself inside the Folly and locked the door; and Banks, with the assistance of a locksmith and a police sergeant from Elmbury, eventually had to break his way in and carry him off by force. He struggled fiercely. His straw hat with the I. Zingari band came off and was trampled underfoot, his tangled mane of long white hair fell down upon his shoulders like the Clarkson wig of King Lear during the storm scene on the Heath. And who knows that he did not believe himself, like that mad King, to be dispossessed of a kingdom – the blurred and yellow tinted kingdom of orchard and meadow which he had contemplated so proudly every day for thirty years from the roof of the Folly, through the broken telescope?

Ruin and Rabbits

Lord Orris had given me permission to shoot rabbits in his park; and I sometimes went up there with a ·22 rifle in the evenings and stalked them as they sat out at the edge of the little coppices. It was more fun than blazing away with a 12 bore.

Weeds and rabbits, as acquisitive as the Syndicate, held joint dominion over the last remnants of the Mad Lord's estate. Nettles and thistles and teasels stood high against the hedges, there was poisonous hemlock at the ditchsides, dock in the waste-ground, ragwort in the Park. Deadly night-shade like lurking adder hid beneath the crumbling stone walls, in the wet meadows there were more fegs and rushes than wholesome grasses, and when the corn began to ripen on the few patches of cultivated land the wanton poppies' scarlet always smothered the gold. And as the anarchic wild weeds multiplied, so did the rabbits; and whatever whole-some thing the weeds failed to choke the rabbits were sure to devour. Priapus was the Park's *genius loci*. 'The Scriptures tell us,' Lord Orris would say, 'that the coneys are a feeble folk. But I ask you: just *look*!' Indeed the fierce fertility of the coneys in Orris Park gave the lie to Holy Writ. They teemed on the face of the earth like mites on a cheese; and before such appalling profusion even the poachers stood abashed, lost heart, and poached no more. 'Pharoah,' said the Mad Lord, 'had his frogs, lice, and locusts, his boils and his blains, but my plague is rabbits. Our crest, rightly, should be a rabbit rampant on a field of weeds!'

'You never shoot them?' I asked him once.

He shook his head. 'I'm no good with a gun, for I can never bring myself to let it off. How often have I set out, burning with indignation, determined to blow the head off every rabbit I could find! I have even gone so far as to *aim* at a rabbit; but then I always think of a dozen reasons why I should not shoot. For instance, how should the death of *one* rabbit benefit me? Here are millions and millions. Again, what if the little beast does achieve five or ten shillingsworth of damage in the course of a year? What is that compared with my debts? Alas, it is a single raindrop to all great Neptune's ocean. I owe my bank five thousand times as much as the hungriest rabbit could steal; I pay those gentlemen over the hill who hold my mortgages five hundred times as much in a year's interest alone. But I don't go and shoot my banker, or blow the members of the Syndicate to bits. And the rabbit has a much more pleasing expression than any of them.'

He smiled and went on:

'By the time I have thought of all these considerations the rabbit has generally run away; but if it has the temerity to stay within range, at the last resort there is always an accidental factor which saves its life. The gun is not loaded; I simply cannot remember to put the cartridges in before I set out.'

... *Musa vetat mori*

Jane, that passionate and exquisite creature, was away from Brensham most of the winter, for she was studying at a School of Aeronautics for her Ground Engineer's Licence. The young men whom she now brought down at weekends were very different from the undergraduate Communists; they had grimy hands with broken nails, and oil-spots on their grey flannel trousers; and their conversation was all about internal combustion engines. On the whole we liked them better than the Communists, for they played darts

earnestly, enjoyed their beer, and had the quiet and confident manner of men who do a job of work and are proud
of it.

In the early spring Jane brought a new aeroplane back to
Brensham. It was painted bright azure so that it looked
more than ever like one of those burnished dragon-flies.
Once more Jane alarmed the village by performing aero-
batics over the church, but her loops were neater and tighter
and she had learned to do slow-rolls; she told us lightly that
she proposed to fly to Australia. She would have preferred
Pekin; but the newspaper which put up the money had
demurred: 'No good at all; China's not in the Empire.'
If she knocked a day or two off the solo record she expected
to get ten thousand pounds. 'And then,' she said, 'we'll pay
off the mortgage and patch up the old house. If anything it
looks more dilapidated than Father.'

The whole village was apprehensive about Jane's crazy
project, and Dai Roberts Postman was even moved to write
her a poem; for he believed that aeroplanes were inventions
of the Devil and was quite certain that she would be killed.
The only true immortality, he knew, was that which lay in
the gift of poets; so he hastened to pay her the ancient
tribute which the Muse has always paid to those who are
beautiful and who die young. When it was finished he
presented it to her without humility or embarrassment; for
although the Honourable Jane was a great lady, he was a
Bard, and the men of his craft had held their heads high
even before kings. 'It iss in the Welsh tongue,' he said,
'because that iss the best language for the writing of poetry.
You will not be able to understand it, but it iss a very noble
poem in honour of yourself, and there are twenty-seven
verses in the manner of Sion Tudor containing altogether
one hundred and eight lines. You will carry it with you in
your aeroplane to the ends of the earth?'

'Of course I will, Dai!'

'Not even the glorious songs of Taliesin,' said Dai
proudly, 'have travelled as far as that!'

The Postman

Dai Roberts, about this time, was having his own troubles
with the Syndicate. Recently one of its members had taken
up permanent residence at the Shooting Lodge. Now in
order to reach the Lodge from Brensham, one had to take
the steep rough lane which led past Orris Manor and skirted
the Park until at last, becoming rougher and steeper, it cut
over the shoulder of the hill to the other side. I met Dai one
afternoon pushing his bicycle up this lane and I asked him
where he was going; for I was under the impression that the
outlying parts of our district had a morning delivery only.
He said that he was going to the Shooting Lodge to take
some letters to a gentleman whose throat he would like to
cut. I laughed and said:

'You don't like the Syndicate, Dai?'

'Sir,' he said, 'they are bloody rats.'

'What have they done to you?' I asked.

'It iss like this,' said Dai, who was obviously glad to meet
somebody who would listen to the story of his grievance.
'Lord Orris iss not, if you follow me, a letter-writing man.
Indeed it iss little but bills and the like that I ever bring up
to the Manor. Now a bill iss not a pleasant thing; and it
wass better for his lordship, and better for me, that he
should not receive his bills too often. So we came to an
arrangement: I would put his bills in my pocket, do you
see, and bring them up perhaps once a week, saving my old
bones, the tyres of my bicycle, and his lordship's peace of
mind. It wass a very fair understanding.'

'Very fair,' I said.

'Ess. Well now indeed, along comes this gentleman to the Shooting Lodge and of course I do not keep his letters as long as I keep his lordship's bills, but sometimes, if there is only one, I do not make the journey in the afternoon. That would be a foolish waste of breath, would it not?'

I agreed.

'Ess. But the day before yesterday the gentleman made a complaint. He went to Mrs Doan Postmistress and he complained, sir, that I had kept back one of his letters for two days. It had come on Saturday afternoon; and I had delivered it punctually at nine o'clock on Monday morning. So I cannot see that he had much to complain of. But Mrs Doan said to me that perhaps I had gone poaching instead of delivering the letter and I must go up to the Shooting Lodge and make an apology.'

'And did you?'

'That, sir, is the point. I did so. I stood on the doorstep with my hat in my hands before a man with a cold voice who said: "You are the postman?" and I said, "Yes, I am Dai Roberts Postman; but I am also a poet," and he said: "I understand you do not like bicycling uphill?" and I said: "Only a fool would like bicycling uphill," and then he said, very cold and bitter, "Very well, Mr Dai Roberts; in order to make sure that my letters are delivered regularly in future, I have taken the precaution of ordering, from London, two newspapers – a morning and an evening one – to be posted to me each day. The one will arrive in time for the morning delivery, the other in time for the afternoon. You will therefore have the pleasure of climbing the hill twice every day *whether there are any other letters for me or not.*" That iss what he said to me, sir, and that iss what he has done. And that iss why I say, *Bloody Rats!* And by God if I could I would like to cut the throats of them all!'

The Oppressors

For a number of reasons, the village had less cause than ever to love the strange oppressive Syndicate. Two small boys, nephews of Jeremy Briggs, had been prosecuted for stealing some green collywobbly apples out of their orchards. In the meadows beyond the Summer Leasow, once Lord Orris', where Brensham boys and Brensham men had been accustomed to go fishing ever since anybody could remember, appeared a notice which said: PRIVATE ANGLING, TICKETS 6d PER DAY, and a self-important oaf from the town was employed to patrol the tow-path and sell tickets on Saturday afternoons and Sundays. And then David Groves, who had been in the habit of ferreting for rabbits in the fields adjoining the railway (for this had long been a privilege of the platelayers and gangers) was caught by an angry keeper and threatened with a prosecution if he were ever found there again.

These actions were incomprehensible to the people of Brensham. The taking of fruit, in a district where in good seasons fruit rotted by the ton beneath the trees, had never been regarded as theft; as Joe Trentfield said, you might as well call it a theft when a kid pulls up out of your hedge some wild weeds for his guinea-pigs. The fish which swam in our river were mostly chub, roach, dace and eels: valueless to the gentry, who generally travelled to Scotland to catch salmon or to Hampshire to throw their gossamer lines over the chalk-stream trout. But the chub and roach gave sport to the village boys with their bamboo-rods, and the eels made a stewing for many a poor man when they were in good condition, at the time of the first frosts. Everybody in Brensham had grown up in the certainty that they had a right to wander foot-free along the banks of their own river

with a rod. Now they were not so much angered as shocked
by the fact that rich men thought it worthwhile to collect
sixpences from boys whose pocket-money was perhaps a
penny a week and labourers who lived on one pound
ten.

As for the matter of the rabbits, David Groves had always
believed that it was part of his duty to keep them down; for
their buries spread into the hedges alongside the railway and
if they were not checked they colonized the cuttings and the
embankments, and might even cause a subsidence on the
line. He earned a few pounds each year by selling them; and
this he regarded as a right, one of the few 'perks' he had in
his hard life. He was utterly bewildered when the keeper
abused him; and he was terrified of the threat of prosecution, for like most men who have always been poor he was
mistrustful of the law, and saw it as his enemy. He didn't
argue or complain; he knew it was no good. 'They turned I
off,' was all he would say. 'They chivvied I off as if I'd been
a good-for-nothing varmint.' He shrugged his shoulders.
He couldn't understand it; for now the keepers were trapp-
ing and snaring the rabbits, and sending them off to
Birmingham market in hampers to sell them at ninepence a
couple. David Groves had never imagined that the gentry
were interested in rabbits or in fourpence-halfpennies.
In the hard rough world as he saw it such trifles were 'poor
men's perks'.

Alfie tried to explain it to him one night in the Adam and
Eve.

''Tis like this, David. 'Tisn't that they're mean because
they're rich, but 'tother way round: they're rich because
they're mean. If you've got a good many thousands and
you still think pennies are important, you can be as rich as
you like in no time. But luckily for us poor men, most
people when they get a few thousands stop bothering about

pennies. If they didn't we'd lose the shirts off our backs before we knew what was happening.'

The Last Crusade

When we heard that Jane was going to fly to London to wait for favourable weather for her adventure, almost the whole of the village went up to the Manor to see her off. There must have been nearly fifty people in the flat field below the house. There were even two or three strangers, and we learned that these were reporters who had come down from London to interview her father. The Mad Lord's vaguely apologetic greeting had greatly puzzled them: 'My dear fellow, you can see for yourself that I have no money! If I possessed anything worth taking you should have it and welcome.' It was some time before they realized that he was under the impression that they were bum-baillies or duns.

While Jane said goodbye to each of her friends, kissed Mimi and Meg and Mrs Trentfield, thanked Dai again for his poem, and tried to explain to the reporters that if they stayed the night at the Manor they would probably get nothing to eat, Lord Orris rode round the field on his old mare and tried ineffectually to clear a gaggle of Gormleys out of the path of Jane's take-off. The old man looked very sad. 'I shall be lonely when she has gone away,' he said. 'And aeroplanes are horrible things.' With a slight sorrowful smile he added: 'I am led to understand that Australia positively teems with rabbits. It will be a sort of home from home.'

At the last moment Jane ran back into the house and fetched a small brown paper parcel which she packed into the cockpit. 'I suddenly thought I'd take Robert with me,' she said. 'His heart might be a sort of talisman.' Then she

climbed into her little aeroplane and started its engines
which crackled so loudly that Rosinante shied – surely for
the first time in a dozen years – and Lord Orris was nearly
unseated. She waved goodbye, Joe Trentfield and I pulled
away the chocks, the wind from the slipstream flattened a
long swathe of grass, and the aeroplane began to move
forward over the bumpy ground. Everybody cheered as it
gathered speed, the last Gormley child scampered out of its
way, the tail lifted, the engine thundered and the sun
glinted on the bright blue paint as the burnished dragonfly
sped along. 'She's off!' cried Dai Roberts; but suddenly the
whole machine lurched sideways, one of the wheels bounced
high off the ground and the opposite wing began to plough
a long brown furrow through the grass. I heard Mimi
scream, and saw a wheel bowling away from the aeroplane
like a cricket-ball, one of the wings broke off it, there was a
long splintering crash and then silence.

Jane was climbing out of the wreckage when we got there.
She was not hurt, except for some scratches on her forehead
and nose. But the bright little aeroplane, that a few seconds
before had seemed as gay and lively as a bird, now sprawled
upon the ground like a dead pheasant crumpled by the
sportsman's gun. Its propeller was broken and twisted, its
nose was buried in the earth, its wings and its tail lay in
tangled heaps about it. Small pieces of torn fuselage were
strewn behind it for twenty yards like the aftermath of a
paper-chase. It was painfully obvious that it would never
fly again.

'What happened?' we asked; and Jane said in a queer
flat voice:

'It was a rabbit-hole. The starboard wheel caught in a
rabbit-hole and she swung out of wind and turned over.'

She began listlessly to pull her suitcase and maps out of
the cockpit, and throw them down on the ground. Last of

all she brought out the brown paper parcel. She stared at it, pulled away a corner of the paper, and suddenly smiled.

'He's broken too,' she said. 'Oh Lord, I've broken Robert!' She handed me the parcel and I could see through the tear in the corner some fragments of smashed porcelain and a piece of grey rubbery substance which had a faintly aromatic smell.

'Poor Robert,' said Jane. 'He wasn't meant to fly.'

Suddenly we heard Dai Roberts shouting loudly:

'Stop him! Stop him! My bicycle it iss that the man iss riding!'

We looked across the field in the direction of Dai's frantic gesticulations; and saw a man on a bicycle pedalling away furiously along the drive. It was one of the reporters, on his way down to the village to telephone to his newspaper.

But Jane got no headlines next day. There is no news value alas, in 'record flights' which fail even before they are properly begun.

The Vultures Descend

Even if Jane's fantastic venture had succeeded and she had got to Australia, won ten thousand pounds, and come back to restore the family fortunes like a fairy godmother in the last act of one of Mimi's pantomimes – even so it would have been too late. The year was 1938; and if there was already talk of war in the Adam and Eve and the Horse Narrow there was certainty of war in the banks and in the City. Lord Orris' remaining stocks and shares, which in prosperous times were scarcely enough to secure his overdraft, suffered a sudden depreciation in common with all others. Simultaneously, to people who were in 'the know', landed property, and particularly agricultural land, began to appear a most desirable acquisition; for whatever happened estates would not shrink to nothing in consequence of a crisis nor England's green acres melt away in a night. Therefore Lord Orris found himself assailed on both sides suddenly; the bank with reluctance and the Syndicate with eagerness called in their loans and foreclosed on their mortgages. There was nowhere else he could go for money; and so, in May, Orris Manor passed into the hands of the Syndicate at last. With it went the weedy garden, the ruined chapel, the muddy moat, and the Muscovy duck; six smallholdings and five cottages; and fifty acres of rabbit-infested parkland with the numerous families of Fitchers and Gormleys, who were encamped upon it in their caravans, and whom the Syndicate evicted within a week.

But like most tyrants, who grow tired from time to time of the taste of too much power and seek to spice the tedious plateful with a dash of magnanimity, they decided at the last moment to tickle their palates with a titbit of clemency. The Mad Lord might keep the Lodge at the end of the drive, which was occupied by his cowman. A room was prepared for him by the cowman's wife, who had been his parlour-maid in prosperous days; and there, in June, he found his last refuge. The cowman went to work for the Syndicate; but he still found time to milk and tend the Mad Lord's five cows and two calves which grazed in the Home Orchard. These, with the orchard itself and his spavined mare, represented the sum total of Lord Orris' worldly possessions. Nor was he likely to keep them very long; for a heifer belonging to one of his late tenants died in calving and as soon as he heard of it he insisted on sending along his roan calf as 'a small gift to compensate him for his loss'. The Mad Lord was madder than ever, people said when they heard of it. Yet his madness, if it was indeed that, was of the gentlest kind; his wits had gradually fallen away from him as the leaves fall from the trees in soft Septembers. His folly was not of grandeur but of poverty; he never imagined himself to be God or Caesar or Napoleon Bonaparte or the King or indeed anybody but the debt-ridden penniless Lord Orris whose fortunes had tumbled down about his ears. He spent his declining days riding about the land which had once been his upon his ancient and Rosinantine mare; a beggar on horseback, he nevertheless seemed perfectly contented and continued, out of his dwindling store, to give things away.

The Mad Lord Discovers Dreamland

'Contented' is perhaps not strong enough a word; for Lord Orris had found in the evening of his life a new pastime which gave him hours of the most perfect and unclouded happiness. It was a simple, cheap and almost childish pastime; and he found it by accident. Meg Trentfield had achieved her ambition at last and 'gone into the films': that is to say she stood in a long queue every day at Elstree or Pinewood to await the decision of some minor tycoon whether or not she was required as an extra, and if the decision was favourable she stood about in the studio all day to await a greater tycoon's verdict whether the brief crowd-scene would be 'shot'. Her sister Mimi, who was a great favourite of Lord Orris', met him one day and described to him in glowing terms this strange and romantic life which her sister was leading; and he said that it was extremely interesting but, for his part, he knew nothing about that kind of thing for he had never been to the pictures. This admission astonished and indeed quite upset Mimi, who went to the pictures at least four times a week; she was as surprised as if someone had told her he had never ridden in a railway train, as moved as if she had suddenly learned that pit-ponies never see the daylight. She immediately prevailed upon her father to lend her his car, and that very evening took Lord Orris to the cinema at Elmbury. When they got there she was disappointed to find that the film concerned gangsters. 'I am afraid,' she said to her guest, 'that it won't be exactly your cup of tea.' Nevertheless, it soon appeared that the film was very much to his taste. He sat up straight and tense in his seat and gripped the sides of it tightly. Several times Mimi heard him gasp with excitement and when the heroine was abducted by the gangsters he sighed with deep despair. When the hero rescued his lady in the nick of time Lord Orris clapped; and when Mimi placed a restraining hand upon his arm at the moment when the shooting started, he clapped louder than ever, and she realized that he was oblivious of her presence and of the audience and indeed of everything except the walking shadows upon the screen. When the show was over and they came out into the daylight he looked exhausted but supremely happy. 'My dear,' he said, 'it was wonderful. That splendid detective! But I never thought he would be in time. When those brutes were torturing the girl, I thought it was all up, honestly! And those policemen on motor-bikes, actually *shooting* at sixty miles an hour. So clever of them. And the brave man who jumped on to the moving train . . . wonderful, wonderful.' Thus he chattered happily all the way home.

Mimi had a very kind heart; and to give so much pleasure, as she said, was a pleasure in itself. She took Lord Orris to the pictures almost every week; so that Joe teased her and called him her new boyfriend. He did not seem to mind what kind of picture he saw. His appreciation was catholic and unselective. Galloping cowboys would make him cheer, star-cross'd lovers sometimes even moved him to weep, he roared with laughter at the comics and whistled the catchy tunes out of the musicals. The only films which he did not thoroughly enjoy were the Walt Disneys, which he thought were too much like real life. This amazed Mimi, who took great pains to explain to him that they were phantasies; but soon she discovered that in this matter they spoke a different language. The nightclubs, gilded restaurants, cocktail bars and Fifth Avenue apartments which she believed to be Real Life, or at least a desirable extension of the Real Life she knew at present, represented for Lord Orris the palaces of fairyland. The lives, the behaviour, and the motives of the characters on the screen were so completely unrelated to anything within his experience that he was able – indeed he was compelled – to regard them as figures in a fairytale, whereas the deliberate parables of Walt Disney were comprehensible and sometimes even painful in their reality.

But of the fairytale, the gorgeous and enthralling fairytale of gangsters and detectives and Nightclub Queens and Dance Band Leaders and Poor Little Rich Girls, Lord Orris never tired. Sometimes, when Mimi was unable to take him, he even went to the pictures alone, riding into Elmbury upon his old grey mare which he stabled at the Swan and standing in the queue with the schoolboys (who were not more excited than he was) to pay his ninepence for a cheap seat. Before long he could recite as accurately as Mimi and Meg the names and the hierarchies and even the matrimonial complexities of most of the inhabitants of the Hollywood fairyland; and in their honour he rechristened his four cows Ginger Rogers, Bette Davies, Mae West and Myrna Loy.

Many a True Word

Autumn came with its old disquiet in the winds that blew through the yellowing orchards; and with a new disquiet in the winds that blew about the world. 'Let us consult the Oracle,' said Mr Chorlton, when somebody pulled the lavatory plug at the Horse Narrow and set up the familiar gurgling, Minnehaha, Laughing Water, in the tank above the bar ceiling. 'For I imagine that is almost exactly the right noise. Now shall we ask it the ancient question: Will there be war?'

'Better ask it,' said Joe Trentfield shrewdly, 'whether it'll be this year or next.'

But before I went to the Horse Narrow again the Munich Agreement had been signed. I asked Joe his opinion of it and he said briefly: 'I never thought I'd live to see us shamed so.' Nevertheless, he was in great good humour that evening because he had a new exhibit to show his customers and with which to decorate his bar. He had lent his old gun to one of Alfie's boys who had marked down a flock of wild duck on the river, and the first shot had blown a hole six inches long in the side of the barrel. Luckily the boy was unhurt; and as Joe passed the gun round for us to see he roared with laughter and demanded: 'Have you ever seen such a comical thing in your life? Might have blowed his finger off!' No misfortune, short of an actual fatality, failed to tickle Joe's catholic sense of fun. 'Bet it gave him a fright!' he chuckled; and Mrs Trentfield, laughing till she shook like a jelly, echoed him: 'I bet it made him jump!'

'Any road,' said Alfie, whose son had nearly been slain by it, ''tis one of them guns that shoot round corners now.'

And then Jeremy Briggs said grimly:

'Pity it's bust. You might need it, Joe, before old Chamberlain makes another agreement!'

We laughed; and none of us dreamed that two years later Joe Trentfield would indeed be patrolling with a shotgun on Brensham Hill.

The Right of Way

For the second time in his life Jeremy Briggs the blacksmith was in trouble with the Syndicate. Long ago he had refused to shoe their horses and had assaulted their chauffeur; this time he had trespassed upon their land and assaulted their keeper.

They had closed a footpath through Orris Park which local men had been in the habit of using occasionally on their way to work; and Briggs had made it his business every evening after work to parade ostentatiously along it until at last he attracted the attention of a keeper, who warned him off. He refused to go; and he then proceeded under the keeper's very eyes to remove and smash to pieces the notice 'Strictly Private' which had been affixed to the gate. The keeper threatened him with a stick; and Briggs, who had a fist like a sledge-hammer, smote him upon the nose.

That was the simple story as it was told in court, and of course there could be no doubt about the verdict. The footpath might or might not be a right of way; that must be settled, said General Bouverie, in another court. Briggs had grievously assaulted the keeper, and he must pay the penalty.

'There is no doubt whatever,' said the General, 'that you are guilty of a most serious offence. Have you anything you want to say?'

'Yes, your Worship,' said Briggs. 'I'd like to say that I

bore the keeper no ill-will; he was only doing his duty. I lost my temper, and hit the wrong bloke, that's all.'

'And who might be the right bloke?'

'Them,' said Briggs emphatically.

'Them?'

'The keeper's bosses. Them as shut the footpath. Them as prosecuted the brats for pinching green apples. Them as has us turned off the river bank. Them—'

'That's enough,' said the General sharply. 'You're not exactly helping your case, and I'm not at all sure whether you are treating this court with proper respect. In fact you seem, in a vague sort of way, to be uttering threats. We are going to fine you ten pounds or a month; if you give any further trouble it will be prison without the option.'

But when the case was over and the court rose he grinned at Mr Chorlton, who had recently been appointed a JP. 'Stout-hearted chaps you breed in Brensham,' he said. 'We could do with some more of them.'

Briggs paid his ten pounds and went thoughtfully home. The matter of the footpath was in itself only a small grievance, but Jeremy had brooded upon it until it seemed to him a microcosm of all the oppressions under the sun, and although the right to pass through Orris Park was only a small and trivial right its importance was magnified in his mind until it became the sign and the symbol of a great Freedom and a larger Liberty. He swore that he would not let the matter rest; and one day when I was driving past his forge I found him in earnest and whispered conversation with Mr Chorlton and I guessed that there was a plot afoot.

Mr Chorlton waved to me and signalled for a lift; I was going back to Elmbury and could drop him at his cottage on the way. As he got into the car I heard him say, 'Sunday, then?' and Briggs with a broad grin said: 'Sunday at half past two.'

The New Unhappy Lords

On the way we passed Lord Orris, who was riding back from the blacksmith's upon his deplorable bag of bones. Briggs nowadays shod the Mad Lord's mare for nothing, because he had come to look upon him as one of the Oppressed rather than the Privileged Classes – a victim of the capitalists, a martyr even to the Big Businessmen. Mr Chorlton, who could never resist making a quotation when one sprang to his mind in Latin or Greek or even in what he called the Vulgar Tongue, turned to watch him ambling down the road and declaimed:

> "We only know the last sad squires ride slowly towards the sea,
> And a new people takes the land; and still it is not we."

He whistled. 'By Jove, it's more apt than I thought! Chesterton's 'Secret People'. Listen:

> "They have given us into the hands of the new unhappy lords,
> Lords without anger or honour, who dare not carry their swords.
> They fight by shuffling papers; they have bright dead alien eyes;
> They look at our labour and laughter as a tired man looks at flies,
> And the load of their loveless pity is worse than the ancient wrongs.
> Their doors are shut in the evening; and they know no songs."

How perfectly it describes the Syndicate!' Mr Chorlton went on. 'And in a way it expresses what poor Jeremy was trying to tell us in court. *Them*, he said. He wanted to hit *Them*; but he didn't know who *They* were, and that was really what he resented. Now I believe he was right; for I think one of the most horrible and dangerous modern tendencies is this growth of what I'll call anonymous tyrannies. You get it in industry – huge combines, trusts and so on; you get it in bureaucracy – a Civil Service that seems to become more impersonal every day as it gets bigger; and now we've got an example of it in the countryside. The Syndicate! You can't hit a syndicate with your heavy fist; and that is Briggs' complaint. I'm with him. In the old days, if a factory owner sweated his workpeople, sooner or later, if things got bad enough, they stoned his carriage or booed him in the street. If a farmer was a wicked employer they burned his ricks. And if a landlord was cruel enough and oppressive enough, they could break his windows or at any rate march up to his house in a body and caterwaul outside his front door.

'Now the point is, they knew who the industrialist was, who the farmer was, who the landlord was. Those people had names and faces, and it was common knowledge where they lived. Even the greatest tyrants the world has ever seen – Nero, Tiberius, Napoleon – were known and recognized, and if you liked to risk it you could have a shot at assassinating them. But this new tyranny is quite different. You don't know where the head of a combine lives, even if you happen to know his name. As for the Civil Service, it's all arms, body and legs, but you can't find the head: if you have a quarrel with, say, the Inspector of Weights and Measures, you can't tackle him about it in the street, because you don't know him from Adam. And it's the same with the Syndicate, "the new unhappy lords". Tyrants

ought to have names so that they can be held personally
responsible for their tyranny. Don't you agree?'

'Absolutely,' I said. 'But what do you propose to do
about it?'

'There's precious little we can do. But I have been having
a talk with Briggs and we've got an idea. In fact I'm not sure
that the latest member of the County Bench hasn't instigated
a bit of "conduct likely to cause a breach of the peace".'

'What's the plot?' I said.

'Come along to Briggs' forge at two-thirty on Sunday
afternoon and you'll see.'

The Secret People

I duly went there; and I was astonished to find the biggest
crowd I have ever seen in Brensham gathered together
outside the blacksmith's shop. Sammy Hunt was there, and
Mr and Mrs Hartley, Sir Gerald and his family, Joe
Trentfield, Mimi and Meg in their absurdly fashionable
Sunday hats, Mrs Trentfield huge and blowsy and in full
sail like a square-rigged ship going into action, David
Groves, Alfie, and a dozen more, with a large number of
children of all ages and a score or so of Gormleys and
Fitchers, fortunately segregated from each other, standing
about and muttering in little groups. Jeremy Briggs, who
seemed to be acting as a kind of Master of Ceremonies, was
wearing a bowler hat and his black Sunday suit, with the
gold watch chain across his waistcoat, which he always
wore at political meetings and on General Election days.
But this was not a political meeting. 'There will be no
speeches and there must be no rowdyism,' he said severely.
'All you have to do is to walk.'

Mr Chorlton, who was chuckling with delight, marshalled

the crowd into a sort of crocodile. Briggs marched at its head, and led us up the lane to Orris Park, where he solemnly opened the gate at the end of the footpath. 'There must be no Wilful Damage,' he shouted. 'All you does is to walk, backwards and forwards, up and down.'

And that is what we did. Our ridiculous crocodile wound its way slowly across the Park to the gate at the farther end, turned round and came back, turned once more, and crawled back at funeral pace to the end of the path again. Nobody interfered with us, though a couple of keepers appeared in the distance, gaped at us, conferred together, and unhappily shuffled away. Backwards and forwards, up and down, to and fro we marched for an hour, until we had worn a noticeable track through the thin grass which previously had known the footsteps of no more than one or two wayfarers in a month. When we had finished we carefully shut the gates; and as we walked home Mr Chorlton in high spirits came up to me and took my arm. 'How's that for the Secret People?' he said with a grin; and once more he quoted:

> '"Smile at us, pass us, pay us; but do not quite forget,
>   For we are the people of England, that has not spoken
>   yet."'

This Desirable Property

The Colonel had not taken part in the demonstration, because he had been suddenly taken ill. Three days later he died.

'They'll have to carry me there,' he had said, vowing that he would never willingly go to church again. And now, sooner than he or any of us had expected, he was carried there and laid to rest. For many months a sharp angina had troubled him, but he had made light of the pain, and had disobeyed his doctor's advice to take things quietly. If he could no longer walk over the hill, wade in the water, lie in wait at evening for the wild ducks that came flighting down from the north with the first flurry of snow, he didn't want to go on living. So he went spinning for pike as usual in September, and walked after the partridges through the yellow stubble-fields; and when the end came it came quickly – he was drinking whisky in the Horse Narrow a week before he died. For months afterwards we found it difficult to believe that we should see him no more. He had been almost a part of the landscape for so long that we missed him as we should miss a great oak beneath which we had played in childhood, and which we had known all our lives as a kindly shade in summer or a thing of rugged splendour when the leaves fell.

In the spring his farming-stock was sold, the piebald horses, the deep-sided dappled Ayrshires, the Gloster Spot pigs, the monstrous Spanish sheep for which not even the dealers were eager to bid. I went to the sale and bought the Colonel's gun and fishing-rod for old times' sake. Afterwards I walked down to the Summer Leasow to have a look at the Heronry; but although last year's nests were still there, black rafters at the tops of the greening elms, this season the birds had not come back. Nor did they ever come to Brensham again, to gladden us with their lovely flight as they winged their way over the river across the sunset sky towards their precarious haphazard homes in the windy tree-tops.

A few weeks later the Colonel's farm itself was offered at auction. Now his next-door neighbour, on the river side, had been Sammy Hunt, who owned the osier-beds and a couple of meadows next to Summer Leasow; and a week before the sale to Sammy's great surprise he received a visit from the same 'long-nosed snooping lawyer' who had first appeared in Brensham after the great frost. This man proceeded to put up to Sammy a rather curious proposition. He began by saying that he represented what he called an 'interest' which was anxious to acquire the Colonel's farm. Next he asked if Sammy was in the market for it, and Sammy answered 'No'. 'Excellent,' said the lawyer, 'then we shall find it easy to agree,' Sammy thought privately that he would find it easier to agree with a tarantula, but he held his peace. The lawyer went on:

'You are well known in the district, and are held, if I may presume to say so, in great respect and esteem. Now my clients – I need make no secret of it to you, they already own the greater part of the farmland round Brensham – are less well known personally and have encountered from time to time a certain unreasonable local prejudice against themselves. Our proposition, to be very frank, is that *you* should bid for the farm; since unfriendly people who might deliberately "run up" my clients would certainly not do so if you were the bidder. If it is knocked down to you, at a price which we will discuss, my clients will repurchase it from you at a hundred pounds more than you gave for it. They will also pay all legal costs. In a nutshell – you get a hundred pounds for an afternoon's trouble. What about it?'

Sammy puffed slowly at his pipe and said at last:

'Would such a transaction be legal?'

'Perfectly legal, sir.'

'Would it be regarded – in a business sense – as honest?' Sammy smiled.

'Perfectly. We should describe it as – er – normal business practice.'

Old Sammy got up and his smile faded.

'I am getting on in age,' he said, 'and if my neighbours

have any esteem for me as you suggest they have it is because
I have tried during a fairly long life to act straight. In other
words I haven't indulged in what you call normal business
practice. Take that answer to your masters; and tell them
we are honest men in Brensham.'

'— Of Interest to Speculators and Others'

The lawyer duly turned up in the saleroom at the Swan
Hotel in Elmbury, and after some brisk bidding the farm
was knocked down to him for four thousand pounds. In
spite of the imminence of war, agricultural land was still
fairly cheap in the district; and the farm was a good bargain
at the price.

'For a client . . .' said the lawyer when the auctioneer
asked for the purchaser's name. Sammy, whose code of
honour was a very strict one, had not yet told his tale; and
he still kept his own counsel, for the lawyer might have many
clients. But a month later we saw an advertisement in the
local paper offering the farm for re-sale by private treaty.
The advertisement was headed: 'Ripe for Development.'
We knew then for sure what we had already guessed: that
the Syndicate had come down off the hill and gained a foot-
ing in Brensham.

PART SEVEN

THE BOMB

Close of Play – Brensham by Post – Brief Homecoming – Good Correspondents – The Fire – Hearts-ease in the Horse Narrow

Close of Play

AND NOW I must write of Brensham mainly from hearsay, for on the second of September we played our last cricket-match and early next day I went off to the war.

It may have been our last match of all upon the square smooth Brensham ground; for the field had been part of the Colonel's farm – he had let us have it rent free – and the astute Syndicate had made a quick re-sale. An aircraft factory, recently built near Elmbury, was growing almost as fast as the mushrooms were in the muggy autumn weather; a site was needed for its 'satellite' which would manufacture small components. The Syndicate took a profit of two thousand pounds which perhaps they patriotically invested in aircraft shares. While we played our last game, lorries full of drainpipes were already trundling past the cricket-field along a new cinder road.

It was a curious, uncomfortable match, and I had a sharp sense of unreality even when I was batting: for once it didn't seem to matter if one hit the ball or missed it. We played four short and without our captain; for Sammy Hunt, at the age of sixty-one, had gone back to sea. Billy Butcher during the morning had got very drunk in the Horse Narrow; and at closing-time, dismally reciting Housman, he had gone off to Elmbury to 'list for a soldier. Banks was busy and important in his police-station, where the telephone rang all day. And for the first time in any-body's memory Alfie had drawn the pubs in vain for 'the boys'.

So we lost handsomely and without much minding. We packed away our bats and pads as carelessly as if they had been the impedimenta of a past life which we were now for ever leaving, hurried to the Horse Narrow for a last drink with Joe and Mrs Trentfield and the girls, and then I drove back to Elmbury to do my packing.

Brensham by Post

Thenceforth for many months I heard only scraps of news of Brensham in frequent letters from Mr Chorlton and occasional ones from Alfie, Joe and Mimi.

The unlucky Trumpet had another new tenant. She was an old woman with a considerable beard who greatly resembled the Witch of Endor, and she had quarrelled with most of her customers including Jeremy Briggs, who had sworn he would never enter the Trumpet again while she was alive. Jim Hartley had been recalled to the Guards and had been unable to make his old uniform come together across his great belly. The Adam and Eve was being re-thatched, but the thatcher had been called up and Bardolph had taken on the job. He was no sooner up on the roof than he grew thirsty and descended to the bar; he'd been at the task four months already and had drunk three hogsheads of beer.

Mimi in a round childish hand wrote: 'His lordship I'm afraid is growing very old and feeble. Ginger Rogers has had a calf.' She told me that Jane had joined the ATA and was flying aeroplanes from the factories to the RAF. The Fitchers and Gormleys had picked upon the Horse Narrow for their usual Christmas melée and had broken a lot of glasses which were difficult to replace in wartime . . .

A few weeks later I had a letter from Alfie addressed in that awkward painstaking copper-plate style which gave me a nostalgic reminder of his familiar cricket postcards: 'You have been selected to play against Woody Bourton at Brensham on Saturday next the fourteenth at 2.30 sharp.' *You have been selected* – as if we ever had the luxury of making a choice, as if we shouldn't have to bribe and browbeat 'the boys' on Saturday morning to fill the last three places in the team! But this year there would be no cricket.

Alfie had laboriously scratched out with a spluttering pen what must have seemed to him a very long letter. He told me that the blossom was coming on well and everybody was crossing their fingers and praying there wouldn't be a frost. Rexy had killed three rats under the poultry-house. Alfie's two boys had gone into the Tank Corps and he would have a job to manage without them.

Then I heard from Joe. The new woman at the Trumpet had suddenly died, and Jeremy Briggs on the following morning had marched into the bar as bold as brass and ordered a quart of beer. Now the place had yet another new landlord; his wife was florid, flirtatious and red-haired and was already known, said Joe, as the Strumpet. As for the Horse Narrow, the bar on most nights was full of Landgirls. They sang songs, and Meg played the piano, and sometimes a few soldiers came in and then there were great goings on.

It was nice, in wartime, to see people having a bit of Fun.

Then, after Dunkirk, I heard how the war's lengthening shadows began to reach out towards Brensham at last. A training aeroplane had crashed in the Summer Leasow and Banks had to guard it all night. Jim Hartley had come back from France looking as if he had been on a ceremonial parade, his buttons all polished and not a speck of dirt on his boots. He had lost three stone; but Mrs Hartley was feasting him on such a gargantuan scale that he looked like getting them back before his leave ended. The Local Defence Volunteers prowled the hill at night armed with pikes and shotguns. Soon they were rechristened the Home Guard, and Joe Trentfield became their captain. 'He makes us run about like schoolboys,' wrote Mr Chorlton. 'To think how I used to watch with Olympian amusement the sweaty antics on field days of the school OTC!'

His next letter told me:

'Billy Butcher was killed during the Retreat. Perhaps he found at last the means of escape from himself which neither whisky nor the Groupers nor Sally Doan could give him. Sally has just had a baby. She will be happy, I think; for the memory of a dead hero is a more comfortable companion than ever poor Billy could have been.'

Brief Homecoming

In the late autumn I came home on embarkation leave and spent one day of it walking on the hill with Mr Chorlton. It was a wet and blowy day, the last of October, and there was doubt and insecurity in the air. As we came down the slope of Orris Park I looked about me and saw the season guttering down into black winter. In the Manor drive my feet scuffled through the dead-leaf-drifts and the air was full of spinning and whirling leaves. The gale snuffed the yellow elms like candles; a little warmth seemed to go out of the landscape as the colours faded from each tree.

The usual desolate fields of sprouts filled the gaps between the sepia orchards. The scene was Brensham's familiar autumn scene, a mixture of dull-green and dirty-brown, but two isolated splashes of bright colour curiously relieved it. Close to the village there was a tawny acre of feathery asparagus-tops which looked like a field afire; and upon Alfie's holding there was a patch of purple cabbage which caught the pale rays of the sinking sun and glowed reddish-bronze. So, I thought, in this winter of our discontent the light and the fire glows stubbornly in our hearts amid the darkness and the desolation!

Mr Chorlton was telling me about the Home Guard and the knives and the pikes they expected to use against the Germans, who would come, we all believed, as soon as the Channel lay still. But the village below us looked, as it always did, snug and secure against wind and weather and whatever else might befall. Mr Chorlton broke off his discourse on the correct methods of noiseless assassination and said: 'I do love our houses, John; they look as if somebody had poured a thick brown sauce all over them' – and, of course, he quoted:

> "*If I ever become a rich man,*
> *Or if ever I grew to be old—*"

and then, falling suddenly grave, he said: 'But thatch is no good against bombs and bullets. My God, how the place would burn!'

I felt unhappy and a bit frightened, because I was going off next week to a faraway battle, I didn't know where. I said: 'I wonder if it'll still be here, when I come back,' and Mr Chorlton shrugged his shoulders: 'God knows.'

Good Correspondents

More letters: single ones reaching me at long and irregular intervals and out of chronological order, batches piled up to await me at the base, peripatetic letters which arrived a year late after travelling halfway round the world, stained and dirty and sweaty letters which had been stuffed into a pocket and forgotten because they came in the middle of a battle . . .

Mimi has married a Pole. Alfie's eldest boy is missing in Libya. David Groves is getting to look very old and ill, he ought to have retired long ago but the railway is short of men, almost every hour the troop-trains and the munition-trains go thundering through Brensham station. The Home Guard had a report of suspicious noises in the night and surrounded the larch plantation; but all they found was a badger in one of the Syndicate's steel traps.

The Trumpet is full of Canadian soldiers flirting with the landlord's wife. It turns out that Mimi's Pole is a Count; so she is a Countess. He cannot speak much English. His name is Pniack, and if you pronounce it wrong he corrects you: 'P silent'. This always sends Joe into fits of laughter. Meg is in Ensa and does a song-and-dance act of her own ever so nice.

Alfie has taken on three landgirls. They're helluva good-looking but they quickly gets the backache dibbling in the beans. The plums were very bad last year: just when there would have been a good sale for them at a decent price. But that's the way it is.

Mr Chorlton is a Corporal in the Home Guard, but

Jeremy Briggs is a Sergeant. Wouldn't care to be a Hun if Jeremy got those great awful hands and steely fingers round the back of my neck! How he reminds me of Hopkins' Felix Randal: '*at the random grim forge, powerful amid peers, Didst fettle for the great grey drayhorse his bright and battering sandal!*'

Sir Gerald is a very sick man, and his arthritis keeps him to the house in the winter weather. He has rigged up his bird-table at last, with an automatic camera which is supposed to take a picture every time a bird alights on the top of the table; but of course it doesn't work.

Sammy Hunt arrived unexpectedly in the village wearing a borrowed khaki battledress. 'The sods had the cheek to sink me,' he said. He roared with laughter. 'The so-and-sos gave me a cold swim.'

Mrs Doan, who is mentally incapable of filling in forms, says she is going to give up the Post Office and the Grocery. 'I had a good schooling,' she snivels, 'honest I did, sir, but them dratted papers makes my head go swimey every time I looks at them, so's I don't know whether I'm on my head or my heels!'

Mimi's going to have a baby. Brensham hasn't had a bomb yet nearer than five miles, though the Heinkels go over every night on their way to the Midlands.

They've cut down the tall elm trees in the Summer Leasow where the Colonel's herons built their nests. Funny how often we find ourselves thinking and talking of the Colonel. He was one of those rare spirits which live on in the memories of everyone who knew them. Mimi and Meg regularly tend his grave in the churchyard. Charming of them, and unexpected; but the Nymphs, of course, always worshipped Proteus, didn't they?

Hitler was over again last night. No bombs here, but it was helluva noisy.

Haunted and hounded by Forms, which have turned her hair grey and frayed her nerves and finally driven her into a state near to persecution mania, Mrs Doan is convinced that every stranger in the village is an Inspector from the Ministry of Food.

Now that the Japs have come in Sir Gerald has gone off to Burma. He received a telegram and left hurriedly next day. He looked a very sick man, hardly up to the journey. He wouldn't tell us what he was going to do; but he said to one of the village children, who asked him if he'd be back for the bird-nesting: 'The King's got a job for me. It may take a longish time.'

Pistol, Bardolph and Nym have all been prosecuted for taking mushrooms from a field which belongs to the Syndicate. Their defence was ingenious. 'They were only bluelegs, your Worship.' General Bouverie: 'Do the police confirm that?' The policeman did: they had five pounds of bluelegs in their basket. General Bouverie: 'I understand that blueleg is an edible fungus called *Tricholoma personatum*. It is never cultivated and I doubt if it can properly be called a mushroom. Case dismissed.'

The Pershore plums has been helluva good; but I've got nurn on my Vics.*

There's a rumour that Sir Gerald was sent to Burma to advise about the blowing up of some dams which he'd built himself in 1920. Nothing very definite or certain about him, but a story that he stayed behind pottering with the fuses and refused to leave when the engineers did, but stood and watched the unharnessed waters roaring into freedom from the prison where he had confined them years ago.

Meg is engaged to Alfie's younger son. He's just been home on leave from Italy. The Army has improved him ever so.

* *Ie*, ne'er'un on my Victorias.

The Strumpet has run off with an airman; and now there's another new landlord at the middle pub.

It's D-Day and still Brensham hasn't had a bomb.

The Fire

And then, when at last I came home to Elmbury and asked in the Swan for the latest news of Brensham, somebody said: 'You'll find it very knocked about, I'm afraid.' 'Knocked about? Surely,' I said, 'it hasn't had a bomb all the war.'

It wasn't a bomb exactly, they told me. One of our Lancasters was struggling home hard-hit after a raid on Dresden or somewhere: the last, or nearly the last, big raid of the German war. Its tail had caught fire, and it seemed to be trying to get rid of its bombs, for one went down in the open country two miles from Elmbury. That brought the townspeople out into the streets; and they craned their necks to watch the bright comet streaming across the sky. As they watched, orange fragments broke off from it, a Leonid shower of meteorites from the comet's tail. There was a terrible white flash which lit the whole town, followed by a sudden darkness and a slow red glow on the northern horizon.

It had fallen in two parts. The tail like a Roman candle gushed fiery particles all the way along the main road between Elmbury and Brensham; the rest of the aeroplane, with some bombs still on board, came down in the middle of the village, close to the Horse Narrow and the church. Then it blew up, hurling a hundred flaming brands upon the dry thatch of the cottages, and Brensham began to burn. Joe Trentfield and his Home Guard, the old men, the women and even the children fought the fires with buckets and stirrup-pumps until the engines got there and saved what could be saved. The firemen said there would have been nothing left of Brensham but for the work of Joe and his men. They had even climbed on to the roofs and scrabbled and scratched at the smouldering thatch with their bare hands.

But I should find Brensham very changed, they told me in the Swan. There was a hole nearly fifty yards across in the middle of it.

No: there had been no serious casualties, though Joe Trentfield was scratched by splinters and Mr Chorlton burned his hands. He was doubly unlucky; for while he was helping to fight the fire in the village, his own cottage, ignited by one of the fragments from the tail, was burning itself out, halfway between Brensham and Elmbury.

Hearts-ease in the Horse Narrow

I had almost forgotten the lovely course and procession of the English seasons; I hadn't realized that it was already blossom-time. When I drove to Brensham next day I was astonished, as I have been afresh every spring since my boyhood, by the greenness and the whiteness and the silver spray of the plum-petal breakers splashing against the lower slopes of the hill.

But in the village itself the trees stood gaunt and bare, with that now-familiar leprosy mottling their trunks and branches with livid patches and streaks. By a freak of the blast two plum trees in the churchyard, and the big apple tree which stood beside the Horse Narrow, had partially escaped; and upon these, even though the branches were broken, there was a defiant outburst of leaf and blossom, and in the apple tree a thrush was singing. 'The apple tree, the singing, and the gold!'

The gilded weathercock on the top of the church spire was knocked awry, there were holes in the church roof and the three poplars were down in the Rectory garden. There was a big crater outside the churchyard, and when I looked up the village street I could count a score of gutted cottages. In contrast to the blackened shells their gardens were bright with tulips and daffodils; and the light winds carried the remembered scent of gillyflowers. The front of the Horse Narrow was partly blown in, and green ricksheets patched the blackened thatch of its roof. I had been told that Mr Chorlton was living there with Joe, and I found him in the bar playing a game of darts with Alfie.

I had expected that I should find a bitter and a broken man; but he hadn't changed at all – in fact, I thought he looked younger and sprightlier. He bought me a drink and I asked him if it was true that he had lost all his books. He nodded.

'And the butterfly collection?' I said.

'The whole bag of tricks.'

I didn't know what to say. He smiled.

'You know, it *sounds* worse than it is,' he said. 'If I had had foreknowledge that it was going to happen to me I am sure I should have killed myself; I should have thought there was nothing worth living for. But now it's happened and I've got over the first shock I feel curiously free. It's rather an odd sensation, when you're over seventy and suddenly you don't have to worship the Lares and Penates any more. Those two thousand books which I used to catalogue afresh every year – wondering to whom I'd lent the ones which were missing! Those rows and rows of Magpie Moths and Blues and Fritillaries – how alarmed I was lest the mites or the damp should get into the cabinet drawers, or an eager schoolboy with his pointing finger chip a piece off a butterfly's wing! Well . . . I can think of them now without regret. Too many possessions clutter up a man's life perhaps; and it may be that I haven't got much more of mine left to live. For the last few years at any rate I shall be very free!'

Joe Trentfield had gone into the back-room to fetch his wife; and now she came bustling out, heaving and swelling like a pouter pigeon, and shouting over her shoulder to Mimi: 'Come along, Countess! Here's an old friend of ours back from the war!' Out from the parlour the two girls came scampering, and I was introduced to Mimi's Pole and Mimi's grubby-faced baby. 'Pniack,' said the Pole, coming smartly to attention. 'P silent.' Joe guffawed. 'Wladislaw's his Christian name,' said Mimi, spelling it for me. Joe said with possessive pride: 'He's a Count, you know,' adding modestly: 'Of course they have a lot of Counts in Poland.'

It was one o'clock, the villagers began to come in for their midday beer or cider and I was kept busy shaking hands. Jeremy Briggs seized me with a grip that nearly broke my wrist. Then Sammy Hunt came in, with his bald head the colour of a walnut, for he'd spent the last year of the war in the Mediterranean. We had drinks all round, and Alfie in the same breath told me that his elder son was just back from a prison camp in Germany, the younger was going to marry Meg next month, Rexy had caught another rat under the poultry-house, and there was a cricket-meeting fixed for Monday to discuss the question of making a new pitch in one of Sammy's meadows.

Now I began to perceive that the changes that had occurred in Brensham were only physical changes: burnt-out cottages, blasted trees, holes in the wall of the Horse Narrow bar. Joe behind his splintered counter was roaring with laughter because somebody had brought him a parsnip with a long twisted root which had grown into the middle of a curiously-shaped potato. He held the conjoined

vegetables up for us to see, and roared: 'Have you ever
come across anything so comical in your life? Have you
ever seen such a sight in all your days?' – and Mrs Trentfield's balloon spinnakers filled with a good steady soldier's-
wind of laughter, and Mimi giggled and nudged her Pole.

And all around me I could hear the familiar talk of the
blossom, of crops and cultivations, of horses, of guns, of
dogs, of cricket. Meg was sitting at the piano and strumming
out her tinny little Ensa tune. David Groves in the corner
was silently and thoughtfully chewing his bait – two hunks
of bread with a lump of cheese and a raw onion which he
peeled with his pocket-knife. There was a game of darts
going on, and I listened with a joyful sense of homecoming
to the old absurd backchat:

'Middle for diddle.'

'Mugs off.'

'Clicketty-click.'

'Hard to bear.'

'Up in Annie's room!'

And there was Sammy standing in his usual corner and
telling the Pole a long story about Brensham's Great Frost.

'. . . Believe it or not – you may get it pretty cold in
Poland – but here we were in the first week of May; I'm
not quite sure whether it was the fourth or the fifth, or was
it the sixth, and the thermometer outside my front door –
I'm not leg-pulling – was showing thirteen degrees Fahrenheit. . .'

Meanwhile Mr Chorlton was telling me the news. The
aircraft factory on the Colonel's farm had ceased produc-
tion, and there was talk of its being dismantled. The
Syndicate? It had been lying doggo during the war, or
perhaps it had bigger fish than Brensham to fry; but
recently the long-nosed lawyer had been seen in the village
again, snooping round some of the ruined cottages. If he

tried to buy them he'd be up against some opposition; for Jane had also been down to the village, and she was going to be married to a rich young man who talked of coming to live at Brensham and putting up a loan free of interest so that the cottagers could buy their own houses when they had been repaired.

'Dear, splendid Jane!' said Mr Chorlton. 'She's still searching for a crusade. But perhaps at last she's found one.'

I overheard Sammy say:

'. . . Well, to cut a long story *bloody* short, there I was, up to my neck in the water, and this huge black shape bearing down on me. . .'

I said:

'Oh, Sammy, I heard you'd been sunk and had to swim for it. How did it happen?'

He looked rather annoyed by the interruption.

'I wasn't talking about that,' he said with dignity. 'I was merely telling the Count here our little tale about the Great Flood. I was explaining to him how I was nearly gored in the water by the Colonel's Ayrshire bull.'

I glanced at Mr Chorlton and he winked; and suddenly it struck me that Sammy had practically forgotten about his cold swim in the North Sea and that Brensham had very nearly forgotten about its bomb. I realized for the first time in six years that war was a passing thing. It had passed; and the searing flames of its passage were for Brensham but another memory with all the other great and little disasters that had come and gone, with the dangerous flood and the withering frost, with the brief uncomfortable midsummer madness of the Group and the stealthy invisible menace of the Syndicate looming over the hill. These came and went and left their scars; but they left also laughter and labour and courage, Joe guffawing behind his bar because he loved to see people having a bit of fun, Jeremy Briggs

fighting for liberty in the clumsy heavy-handed way which
was the only way he knew, David Groves with bent back
still 'walking his length' every day, Alfie in his orchards
saying with a grin and a shrug, 'You can't spray against
Jack Frost,' but doing the tedious job each year nevertheless
because he felt he owed it to his neighbours and his trees,
Mr Chorlton starting life again at seventy and telling me:
'I saw a Cabbage White butterfly today and it occurred to
me, "How exciting! I haven't even got *that* in my collection!"'

No, Brensham hadn't changed, I thought, for all that
mattered of it was unchangeable: the brief beautiful
blossoming, a whiff of gillyflower on the wind, and laughter
and labour and courage, the imponderable, indestructible
things.

Other Pan books that may interest you
are listed on the following pages

John Moore
The other two books in his famous Brensham trilogy

Portrait of Elmbury 70p

The first book in the trilogy

The lively and delightfully humorous chronicle of an English
market town, with its Abbey, its misty river, its pubs, pageants,
hunts and markets.

Crowding this timeless world is a wonderful assortment of
characters : Chorlton the schoolmaster, Pistol, Bardolph and Nym,
three rapscallion poachers. Then there are Effie and Millie, warm-
hearted barmaids, and the yeoman farmers with their midnight
steeplechase, the Colonel who lived for huntin' shootin' fishin' – and
whisky . . .

The Blue Field 70p

The third book in the trilogy

Old friends and new faces join the scholars, rogues and countrymen
of Brensham, with its crooked village street and canted church
spire. Among its rare individuals – as one in their determination to
make life a hilarious, romantic adventure – are those lively landgirls
known as The Frolick Virgins, Dai the hymn-singing postman and
William Hart who claims he is descended from Shakespeare.
William loves Pheemy the young gypsy, not wisely but too well . . .

Picador

Flann O'Brien
The Dalkey Archive 75p

Dalkey, a little town maybe twelve miles south of Dublin, is the setting for such characters as Augustine, James Joyce and a man who is in danger of turning into a bicycle. The deeply religious Mrs Laverty presides over the Colza Hotel. De Selby, the mad scientist, who achieves further fame in *The Third Policeman*, discovers how to make magnificent whiskey in a week.

The Third Policeman 60p

This novel is comparable only to *Alice in Wonderland* as an allegory of the absurd. It is a murder thriller, a hilarious comic satire about an archetypal village police force, a surrealistic vision of eternity, and a tender, brief, erotic story about the unrequited love affair between a man and his bicycle.

The Poor Mouth 75p
Illustrated by Ralph Steadman

Flann O'Brien's hilarious Gaelic novel, translated into English by Patrick C. Power.
'A devastating send-up of Irishry' THE TIMES LITERARY SUPPLEMENT

The Hard Life 75p

Into the household of Mr Collopy come two orphan boys. While Mr Collopy is engaged in mysterious humanitarian work on behalf of women, the boys grow up in the odour of good whiskey and bad cooking. Manus progresses from teaching people by post how to walk the tightrope to running his 'London University Academy'.

Selected bestsellers

- [ ] **Jaws** Peter Benchley 70p
- [ ] **Let Sleeping Vets Lie** James Herriot 60p
- [ ] **If Only They Could Talk** James Herriot 60p
- [ ] **It Shouldn't Happen to a Vet** James Herriot 60p
- [ ] **Vet in Harness** James Herriot 60p
- [ ] **Tinker Tailor Soldier Spy** John le Carré 60p
- [ ] **Alive: The Story of the Andes Survivors** (illus)
  Piers Paul Read 75p
- [ ] **Gone with the Wind** Margaret Mitchell £1.50
- [ ] **Mandingo** Kyle Onstott 75p
- [ ] **Shout at the Devil** Wilbur Smith 70p
- [ ] **Cashelmara** Susan Howatch £1.25
- [ ] **Hotel** Arthur Hailey 80p
- [ ] **The Tower** Richard Martin Stern 70p
  (filmed as *The Towering Inferno*)
- [ ] **Bonecrack** Dick Francis 60p
- [ ] **Jonathan Livingston Seagull** Richard Bach 80p
- [ ] **The Fifth Estate** Robin Moore 75p
- [ ] **Royal Flash** George MacDonald Fraser 60p
- [ ] **The Nonesuch** Georgette Heyer 60p
- [ ] **Murder Most Royal** Jean Plaidy 80p
- [ ] **The Grapes of Wrath** John Steinbeck 95p

All these books are available at your bookshop or newsagent:
or can be obtained direct from the publisher
Just tick the titles you want and fill in the form below
Prices quoted are applicable in UK

Pan Books, Cavaye Place, London SW10 9PG

Send purchase price plus 15p for the first book and 5p for each
additional book, to allow for postage and packing

Name (block letters) —————————————————————

Address —————————————————————————

—————————————————————————————

While every effort is made to keep prices low, it is sometimes
necessary to increase prices at short notice. Pan Books reserve the
right to show on covers new retail prices which may differ from
those advertised in the text or elsewhere